We will
not hang our
Harps
on the
Willows

Bärbel von Wartenberg-Potter

We will not hang our Harps on the Willows

Global Sisterhood and God's Song

Translated by Fred Kaan

A Meyer-Stone Book
CROSSROAD • NEW YORK

1991

The Crossroad Publishing Company
370 Lexington Avenue, New York, NY 10017

Translated from the German, *Wir werden unsere Harfen nicht an die
Weiden hängen: Engagement u. Spiritualität*, Stuttgart, Kreuz Verlag, 1986

Illustrations: p. 66, Good News Bible, Ps. 133; p. 70, photo Bärbel
von Wartenberg-Potter; p. 82, photo Bärbel von Wartenberg-Potter;
p. 86, photo WCC/Peter Williams; p. 100, Selket, Egyptian Museum,
Cairo; p. 105, photo Bärbel von Wartenberg-Potter

English edition copyright © 1987 WCC Publications, World Council
of Churches, 150 route de Ferney, 1211 Geneva 20, Switzerland

U.S. edition, 1988, by Meyer-Stone Books,
a division of Meyer, Stone, and Company, Inc.,
714 South Humphrey, Oak Park, IL 60304

Cover design: Carol Evans-Smith

Typeset in Switzerland and printed and bound
in the United States of America

Library of Congress Cataloging in Publication Data

Wartenberg-Potter, Bärbel von.
    We will not hang our harps on the willows.

    Translation of: Wir werden unsere Harfen nicht an
die Weiden hängen.
    1. Women in Christianity.   I. Title.
BV639.W7W2813   1988   208'.8042   87-34712
ISBN 0-940989-34-4

By the rivers of Babylon we sat down;
there we wept when we remembered Zion.
On the willows nearby we hung up our harps.
Those who captured us told us to sing;
they told us to entertain them: "Sing us a song about Zion."
How can we sing a song to the Lord in a foreign land?

—Psalm 137:1–4

Contents

Foreword

St Augustine says that Hope has two lovely daughters, Anger and Courage. Hope, according to this father of the church, is the greatest among the three theological virtues. In the famous Pauline statement, of faith, hope and love, love is the greatest (1 Cor. 13), but Augustine praises Hope for she tells us that God will work God's will.

It is in precisely this sense that I would like to call Bärbel von Wartenberg-Potter's book a gift of hope for those who are in need of a different heaven and earth. A gift of hope for women struggling, women suffering, women yearning for justice.

The strength of Bärbel's book lies in the fact that she is firmly grounded in the life of ordinary women in European churches and yet dialogues with the women of the two other thirds of the human family. She mirrors the fears and hopes of women from the first world but does so in a candid dialogue with our sisters from the third world. Bärbel does not silence their criticisms of Western feminism. Sometimes our struggles appear to them as a luxury of those who are not forced to fight the greater enemy that threatens the lives of their children through starvation and never-ending militarization. Bärbel listens and responds to these questions, she refuses to think of liberation without that global sisterhood, and so she opens the eyes of middle-class feminists for thinking globally and acting locally.

This is a book of hope. Augustine maintains that faith only tells us that God is and love only tells us that God is good, but hope tells us that God will work God's will. Where? When? With whom? Who are God's allies and co-workers?

The first word of this book is *anger*, this lovely daughter of hope. Anger so that what cannot be may not be, and *courage* so that what must be will be. Bärbel who lost her two children has given birth to these daughters of hope we need above all. Indeed, this book celebrates what a song from the new Peace Movement says:

> We are gentle angry people
> and we are singing
> and we are singing
> for our lives

Dorothee Sölle

DOROTHEE SÖLLE

Preface

In the Alsace, one autumn, the apples were falling from the trees and their soft thud as they fell into the grass was about the only sound I heard, as I was putting together and writing down the thoughts which these pages contain. Some of these thoughts simply fell into my lap, others only became word hesitantly, wrought in the workshop of my thinking. Racism, worldwide justice, renewal of the church — these are themes that have for a long time now made my fingers itch. But this time I was particularly concerned with the issue of women and doing theology in a woman's way, and thus with bringing together yet again questions that have been kept separate far too long. I discovered that it is more difficult, yet vitally necessary, to write about women and the church, seeing it affects me personally — to speak of one's own concerns seems to be harder than anything else; one can no longer hide behind generalizations.

Five years' work and experience as director of the Women's Department at the World Council of Churches have caused a great deal to grow within me. What I put on paper here grew out of conversations I have been involved in during those years, conversations within myself and with others. Many people have spoken to me through their books. This is especially true of people of the Bible, a book that has again come to life for me since I started reading it with female eyes, wide open to the world.

Above all, I would love to engage in conversation with the "Theas", the young women theologians and pastors on whom I fervently count for the continuation and the critique of these thoughts begun here — and for whose sake I put them on paper in the first place.*

But I equally recall those conversations I have had with all the women and men who have not yet found definite names for the new departures signalled in this book.

Apples in the Alsace reminded me of the fact that the Bible associates the apple with the knowledge of good and evil, a

---

* Translator's note: "Thea" (pronounced tay-ah) is a play on German names/ words. There is a magazine called "Thea", edited by a group of women theological students, emphasizing women's theological perspectives. "Thea" is a popular girl's name, "Theo" a boy's.

capacity irrevocably given to us not to waste but positively to apply. "The knowledge of good is bought dear by knowing ill," said Milton in *Paradise Lost*. It is because I needed to find out where we are at present with this knowledge that I wrote what now follows, to unburden my heart.

Kingston, Jamaica   BÄRBEL VON WARTENBERG-POTTER

1. At the cradle of my thinking

Theology out of a concerned heart

Anger stood at the cradle of my independent thinking. My theological awakening began when a couple of elementary human experiences fused with the academic discipline I pursued during five years of my life — theology. The anger was the match that lit a theological fire within me, a fire that has been burning ever since. I was angry at napalm bombs dropped on children's bodies in Vietnam, at bellies bloated from malnutrition in Biafra. I was angry at the "whites-only" notices in Johannesburg suburbia, and at the paraffin smoke destroying the lungs of Soweto blacks. I was angry at the silence of my academic discipline in the face of these events, angry at the lukewarmness of the church in its public statements. I was angry at bureaucratic answers to humanity's questionings, at the betrayal of the poor.

That is how it all started. Anger as the very heart of theology, as a theological discipline, but untaught within the faculty. This is how a new weight-bearing synthesis was formed within me as head and gut interacted. Someone had started rubbing saliva on my blind eyes to heal my short-sightedness and give me an ever clearer vision. A real healing miracle, as I look back. The more I look around me, the more clearly my eyes discern the condition of the world rising up out of the grey bourgeois-churchly mist which I had hitherto accepted as reality.

And I go on being angry.

I am angry at the cold-blooded attitude of the politicians towards the threatening annihilation of the earth, at the depression that is so generally rife among those who are committed. I am angry at the world's gulags where the idea of socialism is being forced to its knees — gulags that can no longer be argued away. I am angry at the Goliaths determined to throttle the Davids of this world, like vulnerable Nicaragua. I am angry at the cages of popular opinion into which they try to shut people up. At the sad emptiness of our worship and the small-mindedness and irrelevance of our biblical exposition. I am angry at the hard dogmatism of the "pious" (my own included), and at the unfaithfulness to this world through a hankering for the hereafter. And more recently, but most profoundly, I am angry at women in church and society being silenced, at the way they are constantly being robbed of their own spiritual and emotional viewpoint.

But anger in itself is not enough nor is it a virtue. It is no more than a starting point I and many other people are going through. The choice of the word "anger" is quite deliberate. Maybe empathy or compassion could have been used, but these concepts did not come sufficiently to the fore; they do not yet have within them any power that will lead to change, even though the ability to put oneself into other people's shoes is a human quality without which we would give sad evidence that our soul is being deformed.

So this is how I declare my point of view, the position I have reached experientially and theoretically: theology — in my case at least — arises out of a concerned heart, and not, as they used to "con" me, out of a cool head — *sine ira et studio*, without anger and ardour.

Although there are many theologians challenging us to an existential concern for people, with most of them this remains purely theoretical. It is impossible to deduce from their concepts where they stand as people. They regard what is human and personal as inferior to what is abstract and general. I have put this narrowing trend of theology behind me and I will not allow myself to be forced back into it. I believe that the synthesis of head and gut bears more promise for the future. In reaching out for theological insights, we, women, will no longer disregard belly and body, our human wholeness, and we will thus firmly stand in the tradition of the Bible. The Bible is fully aware of the fact that all important things emanate from the heart rather than from the head. "Love God with all your heart, with all your soul, with all your mind and with all your strength" (Mark 12:30).

The mind is just one of several channels through which to love God. It is the *heart* that burns, preserves, reaches out, is torn apart, hopes, is full, pure, single-minded, evil or hard; it is the heart that is stubborn, is changed, rejoices, is darkened, hates, obeys, is restless, proud and deflated, is opened wide, decides. God examines hearts and kidneys; hearts are stolen, God's law is written upon our hearts, God is hallowed in the heart. In the Bible, heart, kidneys, loins and womb are places of God-involvement. Similarly, anger is a form of such involvement. But anger is invalid in the realm of the sciences, unless one had enough logical and factual proof to justify its existence.

Those are the rules of the patriarchal game. That is how I let men persuade me to embrace thoroughness — and not altogether to my disadvantage, I must admit. I learnt to see through economic surveys and statistics, studied history and law, accumulated a fairly detailed knowledge about the origin, character and extent of racism. I relearnt biblical exegesis and church history. All these things enabled me to undergird my anger, to convince others that it was real, and to put several stupid ideologists in their place. At the same time, this thoroughness made it possible for me to tackle that coquettish self-stylization, often and readily used by women, along the lines of: "I don't understand anything about politics; it does not interest me either."

"I have got to know it", as a women's group from the USA, "Sweet Honey in the Rock", emphatically put it in one of their songs. "Hungry lips are asking me: Why does this ship bring guns, not bread? I have got to know it. I have got to know it."

The pretended political innocence on the part of many women, which can so easily be exploited — and which *has* been exploited where our German mothers are concerned — the coquetry with ignorance are all part of clichés about women's roles, which like all clichés we need to banish once and for all. "We have got to know it!" We have got to know it, every time the opinion-makers serve up their ideological hash instead of telling the truth, every time our gullibility is exploited — in short: every time our stupidity becomes dangerous. There is no way around it. Recognition of this fact becomes a direct appeal to all women in the dialectics of head and gut not to neglect the head.

During that time of my first anger, a woman entered my life to whom I owe an enormous debt of gratitude: Maria Carolina de Jesus, a black Brazilian from the slums of Sao Paulo, with her *Diary of Poverty*.[1] She did not come to me with analyses or facts and figures for discussion in a patriarchal context, but with the simple description of poverty to which her pen gave a slight, almost poetic touch. She introduced me to the "Director of the Community of Misery" and to the "branches of purgatory", as well as to the struggle, fought day in and day out against hunger, dirt and conflict, taken up every morning in order to secure bread for her children and a better life for all. Once she wrote about a man: "He regards the world with disgust; it is unworthy of a human being." From the filthy slums, Maria Carolina de Jesus, that great teacher of humankind, roused me to revolt when she wrote: "Sometimes I rise up against God, because he has put poor people into the world, and all they are good for is to be a source of irritation to others." No, Carolina, God does not put people into the world as poor. God puts them there as divine image, with dignity, beauty and many gifts. They only become poor through people's hard-heartedness and indifference, through their ignorance, selfishness and ideological blindness.

I am thoroughly fed up with this "blaming-God-for-our-miserable-performance-in-life". The misery of such a theology is crying to high heaven. Why, I ask myself, does this theology they taught me fail — and utterly fail — to credit people with the ability to do wonderful things? Why does it steadily chain people down at the evil edge of their lives, at the very point where they are reaching out into the freedom Christ offers?

"For although in the Christian understanding of man/woman the creation is seen as forming the *ground* of who they are ("and it was very good", Gen. 1:31), it is human sin which is at the *centre*," according to a 1985 position paper on feminist theology.[2]

Weakened and confined within the shadows of eternal guilt — is that really what we are like? Is that God's concept of our bearing the divine likeness? Is humanity's future nothing more than a fatalistic perpetuation of the past? Could we not, instead, make a new beginning, start another history, liberate the future? If I did not believe that we do have a new chance to wake up, leave the old cages of opinion behind us, to turn round, to celebrate Easter, to do something wonderful, then my anger would soon turn into bitterness; and is this not exactly what is happening to many people?

Maria Carolina, by the way, was one of the first feminists I encountered, thanks to the fact that she broke out of the ghetto of women's silence with her little diary, salvaged from the dustbin, thus compelling the world to take notice of a woman's life.

Through experiences like this, and the even more concrete confrontation with misery on the spot, I became increasingly a "bread-obsessed" woman, committing myself more and more to a just redistribution of bread. I started collecting bread-sayings, like "One cannot live on bread alone" (as the well-fed person said to the hungry one), or the Gipsy prayer: "God! if all you are is a swig — come into my throat! God! if all you are is a loaf — come into my belly!"[3] or "Bread for myself is a material matter; bread for my neighbour is a spiritual matter."[4]

My three-year old god-child Hanna once introduced me to a basic theological insight. During a country walk, she suddenly stopped at a wayside shrine which showed Mary bowed down with suffering at the foot of a crucifix. "Why does she cry?" asked Hanna, who is a passionate little eater. I explained that they had taken Mary's child away and killed him. She thought for a while and then said: "Come, let's go home and get Mary something to eat." Eating as a cure for physical and metaphysical pain? Could one say that? The Bible teaches us that the bread which we break is a sign of the coming of God's kingdom.

Later I came to know that marvellous song of the early women's movement, the one about "Bread and Roses" (see p.86). With the synthesis of head and gut this is, after all, the logical way. What is more: it is theo-logical. How I rejoiced, after having been made to *see*, when I discovered at last that at the heart of the Christian church's sacramental act there is a meal, bread shared, wine shared. Throughout history many cords of meaning have been connected to that meal. Among these, my particular church tradition has unfortunately only brought me one strand, that of the forgiveness of sins.

The heart in the head, spirit in the body — these are good preconditions for the birth of theology. This became ever clearer to me and this insight went right against the grain of the entrenched separation between "sacred and secular", "God and world", "religion and politics", "faith and action".

I admit however that there is within me still a preference in favour of the heart and the body. Maybe because they have been so neglected theologically. Maybe, because I am a woman, I am allowed recourse to the intuition of the heart. Maybe because our bodies determine in such a variety of ways our destiny as women.

Practising courage

With anger seen as an activity of the heart, Abbé Pierre has a place here with his insight: "What matters today is not the difference between believers and unbelievers, but between people with a heart and those without."[5] This is why I was and am on a search for courageous people who can train me in the right use of the heart and teach me courage.

Courage is more than a mere frame of mind, more than "having a heart for animals". Out of the human heart, that very centre of our human-ness, there rises up courage — which has nothing whatever to do with foolhardiness. Courage comes from the Latin word "cor", heart. Courage means en-heartenment.

Every human being has his or her own areas in which to practise courage, en-heartenment. For me it was the area of exploring the issue of apartheid.

Getting to know apartheid on the spot, meeting both its supporters and its courageous opponents there and in my own country, and discovering its affinity to racist Nazi slogans, it became a challenge to my courage to give public expression to my opposition to apartheid; for what is the use of keeping such insights within the privacy of our own room? In working through the resulting conflicts, I came to know the manifold ramifications of the activities of the human heart: hardheartedness and heartlessness and faintheartedness, but also courage and goodheartedness, enheartenment and disheartenment, boldness and challenges. Practising courage, my active struggles and my political and theological demands promoted many desk-warriors to attack me through complaints and submissions to the authorities and church leaders. In the battle of words and arguments I realized that I should "cool it". But the verbal shots were nothing compared with the bullets and the beatings the school children of Soweto had to endure.

Somehow such activities came up quite logically and naturally within me. Only occasionally did I need to grit my teeth, not so much in the face of the dirty fighters — with them, the issue was clear — but rather among the people of goodwill, who were full of "understanding" but who felt I was "going a little bit too far", and who urged me to "slow down in the interest of the cause".

I cannot continue writing without saying something about my personal life which has been so integral a part of my theological learning experience. I need to say something about what seemed to so many a great tragedy and for which I have not been able to find adequate words: the death of both my children and the subsequent death of my marriage. The children died of the same illness, from a congenital lack of immunity in the blood. With my second child I lived in the hospital for almost two years until he died.

At the time I had on my wall a post-Second World War poster by the artist Oscar Kokoschka.[6] It portrayed Jesus who, though nailed to the cross, stretches out one hand to the children around him with disturbed and empty faces. One of them reaches for the hand as if wanting to kiss or eat it. On the crossbeam the artist had written: "In memory of the children of Europe who have to die of cold and hunger this Christmas." (I was lucky: I was one of these children, but I did not starve to death.) Next to it, a later overprinting on the poster gave these words from the Bible: "Because I live, you too will live" (John 14:19). It is

"I live and you should also live."

difficult to describe how that image related to my own life at the time. Sometimes I felt as if I myself was nailed to that cross, abandoned to medical science whose communications came across like beatings; I felt deceived and mocked by laboratory findings, with death constantly before my eyes — often wishing that it would be my own death — but it was the death of my child, my children, inevitably. But when? In a month's time? A year? Five years? My children, incapable of understanding any of these things, yet being led like lambs to the slaughter. Blood flowed from their veins and mine, from marrow and bone, in the hope of saving them. The pain and cries of my tormented children were my own, too, for they were flesh of my flesh, blood of my blood. And here was this man who knew it all, bending down from the yellow poster, day in, day out — unable to help, yet helping me each day to bear it. He also saw what so beautifully happened to us in between: the smiles after the nights of death, the devotion of doctors and nurses, and of friends.

And when the children were dead and all our strength had been drained away, the two of us broke up and apart — out of weakness, from loss of loveblood; we breathed our last, irrevocably: exit of a marriage. We were unable to commit our marriage to the healing earth as we had done with our children; instead, we buried it, mourning and guilty, in our hearts. "Because I live, you too will live." One day, through grace, I rose from the grave of pain and despair, encouraged by a yellow poster and by the many people who had helped me to roll away the stone which had barred my way back into life.

What was the meaning of all this? I cannot put a name to it. Only this: it has embedded me more deeply into the Christian tradition and made me more care-ful and (I hope) more honest towards other people. It has given an unambiguous direction to my life: that of resistance and submission. It has enrolled me in the invisible communion to those who have been hurt and with whom I shall for ever feel at one. Life's outrageous demands have affected me deeply and have tested my courage to the limit. Nowadays I think of it almost as a talent entrusted to me: when you pass through deep distress, you experience God in a very special way. The one whom God loves is helped by God to

pull through. [7] How can anyone understand this from the outside? No one should be allowed to say such things except from
within.

And so there was a return of anger, and of resistance against
the pain that people inflict on one another, but which was now
imprinted on the deepest layers of my existence. That poster has
gone on accompanying me, telling me: Jesus does not want to
bring us crosses, nor justify those crosses which others lay on
the backs of their fellow-men and women. Jesus wants to stir us
up to live in such a way that we do not make crosses for others,
but rather that we may liberate those who are being crucified.
And he helps us to attribute human and divine sense to the
unavoidable crosses of our lives. That is roughly how Leonardo
Boff, the loyal, disobedient servant of his church, put it into
words. [8]

Confronting the good

People experience public and personal, outward and inward
courage in their life in a variety of ways. In private life, one
is least able to try and avoid challenges. When it happens
publicly, one can blame others, pass the buck to "those at the
top".

How and where can human beings prove themselves to
be truly human? Are people who temporarily, or on principle, choose not to have a heart really human? Have they
really begun to understand their humanness? I have often
asked myself this question — as a real, and not as a
rhetorical or pharisaical question. "So what in human
beings constitutes their humanness?" asks the singer Wolf
Biermann in one of his songs. [9] How can one find a few
provisional answers to these life-long questions? Susanne de
Diétrich, that small, crippled pioneering woman of the ecumenical movement from Alsace, who travelled all over the
world on crutches to teach people new ways of reading the
Bible, has helped me with her word about "courageous
confrontation". [10] It implies that there can also be such a
thing as a-courageous (heart-less) confrontation, or that
there can be heart-people who are not willing to confront
anyone. Susanne spoke of "courageous confrontation". I
like that term.

On the one hand, there is the confrontation with evil, in myself, in others: racism, sexism, stupidity, heartlessness, brutality, greed, militarism, selfishness, pride, self-opinionatedness, despair. The racist in me, the coward, the heartless one, the proud, comfortable, stupid, security-obsessed one — I can confront that person with her heartlessness. I can declare her guilty, swear at her, unmask her, challenge her to become a better person, plead with her, put appeals or demands to her, hand in petitions, bring pressure to bear on her. Courageous confrontation with evil, inside or around me, is something I have been practising for years; after all, since childhood I had been learning that "we are all sinners".

What is much more difficult is confrontation with what is good, whether in myself or in others. Imagine yourself saying to a concentration camp guard, a torturer, an advocate of apartheid, a protagonist of the arms race, a rapist: "Look, you are good! God has given you a heart. Rouse it. It is asleep. Trust yourself. There is much good potential in you. God has freed, redeemed you, given you a new chance. Come out of yourself. Look after yourself. You are crippled in the cellar of the house of your life, without light. Open the window. Bring yourself to light, God's light, human light. Water the plants of your humanness, your divine likeness. Believe me, it is all there, inside you." That is what courageous confrontation with what is good might look like. Or it could go something like this: "Whenever anger, self-hate and depression overwhelm you, allow yourself to be told: you are good. When lust for revenge comes over you or you feel like pursuing at all cost 'legitimate self-interests', whether as a person or as a group or class, as a nation or an alliance, remember, You are good!" Such courageous confrontation with goodness is much more difficult and is hardly ever practised. After all, we know better: we are evil, and the others are even worse.

When Gandhi went out to confront his armed opponents unarmed, resisting, but only with his courage and determined to appeal direct to the good in his opponents' hearts, this was decidedly the greater challenge. It needed more courage than handling a rifle. Believing in the divine origin of human beings, in the possibility of goodness, in — to quote the Christian tradition — reconciliation between God and man/

woman in our hearts is the greater challenge, also for theology. Jesus stood firm against his butchers; he never allowed himself to be fooled by the evil in them: "Father, forgive them; they do not know what they are doing" (Luke 23:34). If they *had* known, if someone had really managed to encourage the goodness in their hearts, they would have been appalled at what they were doing. Even while on the cross, Jesus said: Come out, you who were dead, you who are good — I will bring you to life. And it did not go unnoticed: "Truly, this man was a child of God," said the Roman soldier (Matt. 27:54).

Courageous confrontation, with the God-given sparks within us, with our godly make-up. How can we entice people to believe in their own goodness? The Orthodox church in its theology devotes particular attention to human sanctification. That's exactly it! Enticement to goodness! What is holy in us is coaxed forth through aesthetics, art, beauty, through paintings, music, through piety and the memory of holy things. At the Feast of the Transfiguration (Mark 9:2-13) the Orthodox celebrate the restoration of God's image in us, the image that had been distorted and damaged through sin. Like Jesus we too can be transfigured, trans-formed to our full divine likeness. The human being within us is enabled to come out of the prison of our inhumanity, to take off our bloodstained shirt, to be bathed, anointed, clothed and crowned by God with the crown of humanness. God confronts us with the potential implanted in our own heart: love of our neighbour, love of our enemies, justice. That is what Jesus made possible; in this way our souls are made whole, are saved.

Sanctification is a long and patient process and people have devoted their poetic gifts to this task, like many great Russian poets, Dostoievsky, for instance.

As "natural" human beings we follow our own survival instincts like animals. (Though I must say that I find it increasingly difficult to look down on animals: they only kill to eat, not out of a desire to torture, nor for money, or in the form of mass murder. Only human beings are killers.) Humans touched by God discover their godly — and hence their genuinely human — sides. But God-touching-people takes place preferably in human shape. Both the Old and New Testaments tell of that. As do Tolstoy's legends: "One day, God arose and, dressed as a man, a woman, a child, knocked on the door of a poor carpenter…" Recognizing God in the form of each woman, each man, each child who knocks on our door, and treating each of them as if he or she were God, is the real test of courage and of our faith:

when God comes
comes again:
maybe an Indian this time
a Philippino
or a Bantu (what do I know?)

when God comes
comes again:
maybe a woman this time
or even woman-and-man
a couple

when God comes
comes again:
maybe in the many
the new society
where justice dwells

when God comes
comes again:
maybe the city of God
the land of the goddess of reconciliation
between people and nature

when God comes
comes again:
from one end
of the earth
to the other

Kurt Marti[11]

The task is not to miss out on the one person behind whom God — coming again — could be hidden. The task is not to miss God in *any* human being, or in creation.

Communion of women-saints

For this kind of courageous confrontation we need each other, we need a community. We must bear in mind that all people are able to be challenged to give an account both of the evil and of the good that is in them. Everyone matters, no one is to be written off. There are no absolute enemy images. Every human being merits being confronted. The people who confront us are as important as those who support us. Taking these risks implies that we do not go it alone. Solo efforts are too often deadly. Thus the theological premise is changed from the theme "the individual before God" to that of "together with God". This is a fundamental and far-reaching shift in emphasis.

The sphere of my life has constantly widened itself. My horizon went on being extended across the whole inhabited world, the oikoumene. In the process I also discovered — at last! — the women. For one who, like myself, has been pursuing her good fortune in a men's church, among the "fathers and brethren", this turned out to be — as in so many women — a slowly progressing advance towards "decolonization". The occupation forces in my head were being pushed back, beginning to withdraw. They retreated in the face of the developing power of my own independent thinking as a woman. The "parched stretch of feminine 'I-loss'"[12] had been overcome.

Emmeline Pankhurst (1858-1928), one of England's great suffragettes, describes in her autobiography how the example of the abolition of slavery somehow raised the thought in her, which suddenly made her stop in her tracks — nonplussed: Yes! when slaves are set free and given the right to vote, then why not the women, too? Her conscience was sharpened on the whetstone of the slavery issue, and went on from there to focus on the women's issue. The struggle for the status of woman was a matter of justice, as were the issues of slavery and racism; so it was for me.

The denial of elementary justice to women, especially in its more subtle forms, occupies and outrages me.

Should whites speak up for blacks? No! Should men speak up for women? No! Should blacks be given less education than whites? No! Should women be given less education than men? No! Should women be addressed as brothers? No! Can one justify racism biblically? No! Can one justify sexism biblically?

No! And so on. The facelessness, the namelessness, the lack of self-worth, the lower wages, the subjugation to the worth of "others", the need for being separated in order that we might find our own worth — all these things are typical of the basic pattern of all oppression and liberation.

Today we are right in the middle of the high seas in our search for our identity as women, but also as men. The waves are surging. Who *are* we in fact? What is female? What is male? What is it that we women want, or do not want? What is it that we can do, or cannot do — in our love, in the church, in the family, in politics, in the professions, in the arts, among sisters? Are women the better human beings? Are they more peaceable?

These are the nuts we have to crack. On some of the issues we are quite clear, but there is much that we do not know. How else, though, could it be? At its most fundamental level, the twentieth-century women's movement is a cultural revolution which has only just begun. Patriarchy is bankrupt. We know this from the ecological, economic and armament crises around us. Women and men are both looking for a way out, into the future. Women have become an immense driving force in these things. So my experience in the oikoumene and at home tells me.

True, I have stopped believing that one can explain or change the world from one single point of view, whether it be the exclusive standpoint of the doctrine of justification, or of economics, or of racism or sexism. Ecumenism has shattered my tendency towards any absolute conception of the world. The monster that is tormenting the world has too many heads. I have — I hope — been cured once and for all of falling for exclusive patterns of explanation; there are too many deforming forces about. But there are also many different healing forces, rather than any single one, at work. We must apply them all together, for the earth is mortally ill and needs many faith-healers and whole-makers. Meeting the globe's inhabitants has made it very clear to me in how many ways the lines of God cross over from east to west, from north to south. People with a heart are to be found everywhere, women, men, children, blacks, whites, yellows, greens, reds, old and young.

Despite this, I should like to make here a declaration of confidence in support of the global sisterhood, a credo for the *communio sanctarum* (please note the need to prune even Latin of sexist language!), the communion of saints — in this case women. My confidence in the women of the world and in the churches has grown with every succeeding year. I am talking about little saints, the Joans of Orleans and of the stockyards* and slums, the living and the dead, sisters and mothers, the physical and spiritual ones who on the streets, outside military barracks, in colleges, parliaments and synods, at the typewriter, at the cooking pot and the sickbed, in the field, the factory, the jungle, in the dirt and poverty, practise "courageous confrontation": I have learnt to respect my sisters, to love them and to expect great things from them:

— The women in Rio, the theologians who together celebrated communion, Catholic-Protestant, and who were reprimanded from the top not for denominational reasons, but because the celebrant had been a woman.
— The marvellous conspiracies against patriarchy, when we are among ourselves and are able to laugh together as on our sunlit balcony we are cooking something up, something courageous.
— Or that young woman at the lectern in the Central Committee meeting: beautiful, intelligent and more competent than most of the men present. Fair, and with diplomatic shrewdness, she has a talent for putting the courageous confrontation of the World Council of Churches to the vote — and my heart swells with pride, happiness and gratitude at having such a sister.
— The dark laughter of the friend who had already been dead three times, clinically dead, by her own choice, yet who had been restored to life and who today is full of courage, like no one else, capable of bearing burdens, full of depth and spirituality, a woman whom I took to my heart as soon as I set eyes on her.
— The little prostitute with her rotten teeth, who was showing me around the slums where she is carrying out literacy work among women in order that they may be able to work out their own thought in defiance of the church's condemnation of their sinfulness.

---

* Translator's note: St Joan of the Stockyards — a play by Bertolt Brecht.

You know, there are so many of them: *communio sanctarum*, as varied as the earth-circle itself, and yet they are able to discover, however painfully slowly, the things they hold in common. In that very struggle it is clear that they have a heart, and wounds, that they are angry and determined to discover something new, something better than we have at the present.

Beggar

Beggarwoman am I,
if you do not enter into my queendom.

I could be a queen
if I could give you what makes you rich.

But my kingdom is not yours.
and so we both remain
beggars — comforting one another.

2. Declaration of love to the church

Inner fire

"I have loved you since long and, to my own delight, wanted to call you mother and to sing you a simple song..."[13] With this loving desire in his heart does Hölderlin, the poet-brother, begin his ode to the city of Heidelberg. Sometimes I think of the church in similar hymnic tones, that great world-wide church to which my own church also belongs. I think of the church that trained me as a child to sit still in hard pews while the "pure word of God" was being expounded to us; where, through its Protestant pietistic hymns and Bach chorales, I was introduced to a new world of faith, and the passion and the seed of the kingdom of God and its justice were being sown within me. Slowly but ever more surely this kingdom of God detached itself from its intangible hereafter-existence and quite concretely came to life, down-to-earth. Extricating myself from the fetters of my tradition, I discovered that I can participate in God's kingdom not only in the world to come, but I can also, as Christoph Blumhardt put it, down here "in my very tasks prepare the way for the kingdom of God",[14] with my work towards a better kind of justice than we have today, towards a greater will to peace and love for the enemy. It was in this very church that the ever deeper desire lodged itself within me not to let my life be used as a tool of injustice, but, as Paul said, "to yield our bodies to the service of righteousness" (Rom. 6:19).

So this is how I would want to start my declaration of love to the church: "I have loved you since long and, to my own delight, wanted to call you mother and to sing you a simple song", this church which, according to the Augsburg Confession, "is the assembly of all believers among whom the Gospel is preached in its purity and the holy sacraments are administered according to the Gospel",[15] the church — that gathering of children, women, men, bishops, lay people, ministers, handicapped people, foreigners, youth, action groups, women's groups; that community of all those for whose life this old book, the Bible, has meaning and for whom the way Jesus lived and died is not merely a historical coincidence.

All of them have helped me to grow, humanly and spiritually — even, and particularly, in the struggle, the sorrow and the defeats through which I have been formed in a special way. And so this very special love declaration, so personally meant, is to all of these.

For the church, this communion of people, carries within her womb the irresistible power of the unarmed truth[16] of Jesus about God's entry into the world, about a God who has stopped sitting on heavenly thrones and looking down from afar on the helpless to-and-fro of his/her creatures, but who instead "minded our business" in order that we might know how to be truly human beings, through our bond with the God of love who desires nothing but our temporal and eternal happiness.

This church, however, also brought me up with many forbidding phrases, with many truths for the head and with much moralizing through which my physical existence as a woman came to be hurt.

It is this very church that often tortures and irritates me, and embarrasses me because of its legalistic austerity, because of its unfaithfulness to this world in favour of the hereafter, because of its hopelessly well-balanced statements where matters of peace and justice are concerned.

It is this very church which does not move a finger as it simply stands by and watches the walk-out of rebellious women from its ranks, without recognizing the deeper meaning of and search for the absolutely essential renewal of our male brain-religion.

My love towards the church is as vulnerable as any other love, full of doubt, conflicting thoughts and feelings, but it is real. I cannot always be sure that this love finds a response; whether the church loves me, too, and is willing to bear with me and have me. This love is therefore always the outcome of hard work and grace. But the inner fire that keeps it aflame could never be extinguished, whether through the critique of rationalism or through the bureaucratic character of the church, not even through feelings of shame about us as Christians.

Dream images of reality

Martin Luther King gave a new direction to the black struggle in America when he said: "I have a dream." Dreams are often the designs of tomorrow's reality. Dreams are capable quite suddenly to put before our eyes unexpected images which cannot be controlled and which contain their own truths.

With the eyes of my memory I see the image of a small kitchen in San José, capital of Costa Rica, in one of the poorer sections of the city. Twelve people have gathered there for Sunday worship: six women, four children, two men. With the help of a footstool with a clean table cloth, the kitchen table has been transformed into an altar, with a cross and a few dusty artificial flowers on it. The young man opens the service with prayer and reads a story from the gospels. Then all of them begin to voice their thoughts about the story: what they have discovered in it, where they have recognized themselves in it, what in the story is similar to their own situation, what it says to them for the coming week.

I follow the movements of the Holy Spirit who out of the mouths of the children and women from the slums brings forth power; a church full of gentleness becoming a cell of uncompromising hope for life.

In my dream there appears a group of black women singers, "Sweet Honey in the Rock". They sing before a mainly white audience at a women's conference. In that somewhat stilted atmosphere of goodwill and zeal their songs unequivocally conjure up before us the image of black mothers who are fighting for survival, who, surrounded by rats, unemployment, alcohol and drugs, are trying to keep a family together. Their song is addressed to the white man who controls America:

> You chain my body to dope,
> blow my mind up in smoke.
> It's a wonder I can still sing my song.
> Alcoholism is doing a lot of your killing.
> If I forget to pray once I'll be gone. [17]

Without praying, the power to resist the destruction of the soul is being lost; spirituality as a source of strength for life this side of the grave, as a wellspring of human dignity, as a way of insisting that human beings are more than what others in their greed and racism are trying to make out — all of that would be lost without prayer.

In my dream I see a man with a clerical collar in an Asian country together with a group of women clearing up after a church social. He tells me with a grin, while doing the washing up, how today he had chosen the better part of his office: service rather than administration — he being a bishop. Here was a church where office does not lead to hierarchical behaviour and where everybody engages in service without question.

After such experiences I stick a new marker into my map of the kingdom of God: "That's where I came face to face with it", I tell myself in those moments when both vision and courage are threatening to desert me. It is about such churches and people that I dream, when I dream about the church. I know that we have churches like that in Europe, too, and I am excited about that and I rejoice in belonging to them. Those are the churches I should like to hold up as an example, lose no time in taking them home, to show the people in my home church. I would love to help bring to an end our quarrels, forget our self-righteousness, help remove the rubble, the asphalt of our dogmatism, and make a new start all over again, in all simplicity, direct, with new images of God's kingdom in our hearts and new designs for the church in our heads.

This is what we need: new images by which to orient ourselves, which help us to lose our fear of change, whose intrinsic truth we are able to trace — images which are precisely what they claim to be and which give us courage to tackle this task.

Protestant heritage: pro-test

There is no place where one can more profoundly experience who one really is than in the ecumenical movement, that mirror showing us so clearly from which ecumenical province we hail. It was in this mirror that I discovered the two churchly traditions which had contributed particularly to my formation as a twentieth-century West German woman. With the help of these traditions I should like to try and unfold my dreams about the church.

The first tradition: I recall that in my parental home in the Palatinate we called ourselves Protestants (not "Evangelisch"). * Both the name and the tradition spell commitment in two respects. We won the name through a protest by Lutheran princes and cities at the 1529 Diet of Speyer, at a time when an official imperial decree might well have put a stop to the spread of the Reformation.

---

* Translator's note: most German regional churches are called "Evangelisch", more in the sense of non-Roman Catholic than of our "evangelical".

To this rebellious protest, so essential to the faith, we Protestants are, and want to go on being, committed. At times when we are being sadly intimidated and when courage to stand up and be counted is missing, I often tell myself: "Bärbel, you are a Protestant."

The other aspect concerns the content of our protest; it is a *pro-testari*, as it says in Latin, testifying *in favour* of something, "pro", for, as a clamouring to be heard in the form of protest, such as a pro-test in favour of a better understanding of the gospel, in favour of a greater credibility on the part of Christians, in favour of the church's renewal, of the kind of Christianity that takes its cue from the kingdom of God.

Pro-testing, the breaking open of rigidity, dogmatism and wrong developments have been typical of all significant movements in the church: the clearing up, removing the rubble, throwing out thoughts and actions which, because they have become fossilized into ritual, are no longer capable of conveying things that are alive. It is this making room for something new. Of course Jesus himself is also reported as having been involved in this pro-testing and clearing up. He cleansed the temple with a holy anger and direct action (John 2:12-22).

It is well worthwhile accepting this passage, which has been so badly neglected, as part of our heritage, and to put it into practice — following Jesus' example.

Jesus cleansed the temple which had become a robbers' den not so much through sexual promiscuity or a wishy-washy religious life as through pious profit-making. He protested not only against the place where it all happened, but against the thing itself. What he castigated was the soiling effect of religiously sanctioned profiteering. Religion as a profitable business has for many people always been a stumbling block: the misconception that it is possible to secure oneself a place in heaven through buying it, through life-long instalments; as if one could actually purchase the meaning of life or a relationship with God!

Sometimes I imagine the scene: a Jesus, a Luther or a Lutheress, throwing the files and shareholdings of the church's money-changers on to the street, putting a stop to the Tetzels of all centuries, to the clever pedlars of salvation, to the brokers of assets.

Many a renewal has been sparked off with the attack on the despicable Mammon and the profitable religion-business. I think that those of us who come from one of the richest churches in the world will not be able to get out of this. Is it conceivable that we might not need the temple-cleansers and throwers-out, the radical putters-up of theses, because *we ourselves* have already begun to set about reordering this matter of the church's wealth? In the oikoumene throughout the world, there are many churches — in fact, the majority of them — which are free from state-dependent structures ("Volkskirche") and the guarantee of church taxes. Our church is an exception. It should be possible to find a different structure and to begin at last to think the unthinkable: to find alternatives and new ways and means of making the service of the gospel — in the literal sense — less expensive.

Pro-testing, clearing up, removing rubble, cleansing the temple, all this is part of my heritage.

The second tradition under whose obligation I live is that of the will towards the constant renewal of the church. As the heirs of the continuing Reformation in the seventeenth century put it: *Ecclesia reformata et semper reformanda.* Surely this can only mean that we submit ourselves readily and willingly to a constant cleansing process as a natural part of our Reformed heritage. This means that we do not bury or hoard our tradition like a talent entrusted to us, but that we keep looking at it very critically in order to see whether in changed circumstances it still conveys the same message that was originally intended.

Under the heading *ecclesia semper reformanda*, the church which is constantly renewing itself, I should like to single out three areas that could do with a theological cleansing. They form an unholy trinity which has come to tower over us, heavy with the centuries, theologically well-founded, legitimized by the fathers:

— a wrong understanding of justification through works in our theological thinking;
— the flight into otherworldliness;
— obedience to the state.

Whenever I tell people that I am a minister of a Lutheran church, many of them ask me: "Why are Lutherans so opposed to changes in the world?" To which I am unable to give a reply.

Lutheran theology has quite unhistorically interpreted Luther's attack on the kind of piety which, instead of arising out of a God-inspired life, put the accumulation of pious achievements at the centre, thus turning justification through good works into a negative dogmatic fetish within theology. The very expression "justification by works" in theological parlance has deteriorated into a mere formula which tends to be used to turn away from courageous but unpopular activities in the church. By contrast, in the secular world, we indulge in an unbridled justification through diligent work and achievement (*Leistung*) which says: "I am justified because I am successful"; with our negative use of the thought of justification through works we have theologically and practically discouraged Christians from becoming socially involved.

But the thing is that, living as we do today with a 450 year-old history of Lutheranism, and having accumulated experiences with Reformed theology, we discover that the application of theological formulae has to take place in the context of the reality in which we are living. Seeing that we are living in a secular society that is totally dominated by justification through achievement, we, as church people, should not so much bewail the exaggerated sinfulness of pious achievement as a lack of a relevant and bold *praxis pietatis*, a lack of discipleship which, according to Bonhoeffer, "does not recognize our distinction between the outward and the inward... that a good 'disposition' can take the place of total goodness is quite unbiblical".[18]

Seen historically, where has the rejection of that justification through good works led us? To the handing over of the Jews into the hands of Hitler and his henchmen; to the surrender of creation into the hands of the technocratic manipulators and lobbyists; to a fatalistic shutting of the eyes in the face of deaths through hunger and torture in the world. It has led to a situation where the expression "improving the world" has become a dirty word in our synods; it has led to the idiocy of branding the theft of Coca-Cola bottles from a supermarket by youngsters as a sin, while declaring that the exploitation of the third world is part of the legitimate mechanics of a free-market economy.

This is why a text like "Therefore, my brothers, I implore you by God's mercy to offer your very selves to him: a living sacrifice, dedicated and fit for his acceptance, the worship offered by mind and heart" (Rom. 12:1) could only be understood as a challenge to die heroically in the war of patriotism. But, of course, Paul had something quite different in mind, namely making body, and life itself, available in the service of the God who cares about the weak, whose robe is woven of justice. What he has in mind is the total commitment of God's co-workers, who will dedicate their power, love and time to the service of God's justice and peace. A man like Luther was able in his time to fight against the business-minded marketing of the salvation of souls by saying: "Lord, you look upon the strength of faith in our hearts, rather than on good works." But who is going to tell the pious Christians of today who live out the power of faith in the quiet privacy of their souls' closets that faith without visible public action is dead? That the church should not fulfill religious needs but rather preach the gospel; that the Christian faith isn't the icing on a cake, but rather salt and yeast and a response to the question: "How shall I live my life?" *Praxis pietatis* is the new/old theological standpoint, or rather point of departure. It is based on Jesus' words: "Not everyone who says to me 'Lord, Lord' shall enter the kingdom of heaven, but they who *do* the will of my Father who is in heaven" (Matt. 7:21).

The second element in need of a theological cleansing is the pious love of the hereafter which is often perverted into a kind of other-worldly escapism.

Bonhoeffer said: "There are people who regard it as frivolous, and some Christians think it impious for anyone to hope and prepare for a better future… in resignation or pious escapism they surrender all responsibility for reconstruction and for future generations."[19] Yes, there does exist a terribly impious yearning for the hereafter, which is identical with being unfaithful to this world which God has entrusted to us. This unfaithfulness to the present world is reflected in phrases from an official church statement on nuclear armament, such as this one: "Questions in people's minds about the survival of the world, however important, should not be confused with questions of faith and doctrine."[20] Or in utterances like this one, by an educator of theological students: "And so a nuclear war under the world-rule of God is to be feared much less than careless living under human rule."[21] Once such utterances have become incorporated in our church history books, they will throw a sad but unmistakable light on our unfaithfulness to this world through our concentration on the world to come.

The third element in this unholy trinity is what for us in Germany is such a deep-rooted need to be obedient to the authorities. This obedience takes the wind out of the sails of any courage to stand up for one's beliefs. The two kingdoms doctrine, through which Luther attempted to create a new order of relationships between the authorities (who were — let it be noted — well disposed towards him) and the church, should be "unpacked" in a different way for this secular post-Enlightenment age. It is a formula which, having come under different circumstances, is not now very helpful in clarifying relationships in the context of a pluralistic democracy. When J.S. Bach in one of his cantatas uses the text: "The authorities are God's gift, yes, even God's own image", it is hard to apply that unquestioningly to the policies and actions of our political leaders of today. We Germans who have such a long history of "having to learn the strength of obedience"[22] should today also learn again the strength of disobedience.

Pro-testing and *ecclesia semper reformanda* are our heritage. If the church is to remain, it cannot remain as it is.[23] Why is a phrase like this so difficult for the churches of the Reformation? Today, as never before, we have the opportunity to participate in different forms of being-the-church, through the ecumenical movement, to let ourselves be inspired to try and share in new models and new courage within the worldwide Christian family. Admittedly, this is difficult for us, for we are so accustomed to thinking that we have to stand guard over a kind of theological Nibelungen treasure.

Just as "one cannot use the gospel to escape from the demands of the gospel",[24] one cannot hoard the Reformation without being constantly surrendered to it. This is why I long for a church in which I can protest without being afraid, in which we are wanted and trained as pro-testants, for only in this way can the church itself be steadily renewed and the Reformation be kept alive.

Mother-church, conceiving and life-giving

After all this clearing up work, I want to come back to those dream images of which I spoke at the beginning. The church has in the course of its history lost or given up several of its beautiful and good self-images. The discovery and rediscovery of ancient and beautiful symbols also bring back the images which these symbols are meant to represent.

"I have loved you since long and, to my own delight, wanted to call you mother," said Hölderlin. The old church fathers used to call the church "mother church", as the Orthodox do till this day. Alongside the image of the community of the faithful, as portrayed in the disciples gathered around Jesus at the last supper, this image of the church as a mother has its own rightful place. The fathers of the early church, who were so actively involved in expelling what was feminine from the sacred places, nevertheless retained some awareness that one cannot live completely without it in the realm of symbolism. To them the church was like a mother, feeding, protecting them, and giving birth to truth, refuge and comfort. In entering the darkness of the catacombs they returned to the mother's womb, into that protective space, the silence, the life-saving refuge from sword and lion. In the sounds of litanies and canonical prayers people found a kind of comfort that was different from that contained in the pure reason of the preached gospel; perhaps the comfort with which a mother comforts, with a song, or a gentle caress.

Like a mother hen the gothic domes gathered the faithful under their wings. Spirituality, too, was filled with different experiences of being-with-God, being-at-home-with-oneself. You were not just a sinner before a judgmental God, not just an individual, anxious about the salvation of your soul. Those who were there were simply the many poor, tormented or happy or very ordinary people who entrusted themselves to the female half of God, the sheltering, protecting, comforting God who cares for her children like a mother. Of course, wherever the mother-church became like a matron who alone was able to save, grabbing everything for herself, including the sole right to forgive people's sins, her children quite rightly ran away from her as they rose up out of their medieval dependence.

But under the iconoclastic radicalism of the Reformers we lost the meaning of such symbolism, or of any symbolism for that matter. We Reformed people are, as Fulbert Steffensky put it so well in his beautiful book *Celebration of Life*, in the first instance a church of theologians — stern, rational, a brain-religion. A father-church, determined more by the paternal strictness of its theologians than by motherly forgiveness and forbearance. Yet the recapturing of such an image and of such symbolism is not all that alien to the thought-pattern of the Reformation. If it is true that we can recognize God in the love bestowed on us, as it says in John's letter: "Though God has never been seen by anyone, God dwells in us if we love one another; God's love is brought to perfection within us" (1 John 4:12), then it may be equally true that many people experience such love in the first instance in the form of a mother's love and faithfulness to her child: being accepted, reliability, patience readily given, caring — without having to merit all these things and irrespective of whether it be a beautiful, healthy, nasty or restless child. All of that is a reflection of what we say about the grace of God: yes, it is pure grace, with no strings attached.

Such acceptance is not just the privilege of mothers. This is how Jacques Lusseyran, who became blind in a childhood accident, writes about both his father and his mother:

> My parents spelled protection, trust, warmth. When I think of my childhood, I can still recapture that feeling of warmth above me, behind me, around me, that wonderful feeling of not yet having to live on one's own account, but rather relying totally, body and soul, on the support of others who are there to take over one's burdens. My parents bore me up in their hands... I walked unscathed between dangers and terrors, the way light passes through a mirror. That is what I would identify as the happiness of my childhood: this magic protective armour which — once you have been clothed with it — keeps you safe for the rest of your life. My parents — they meant heaven to me. Not that I was able to put that into so many words, and they did not articulate it either, but it was quite clearly there. I just knew (and that from very early days, I am sure) that there was another being who accepted and addressed me through them. Not that I called this being God — my parents did not speak about God until much later. I did not even put a name to it; it was simply there, which was much more important. Yes, somehow behind my parents there stood someone and mum and dad were only commissioned to pass this gift on to me first-hand. It was the

> beginning of my faith and it explains why I have never harboured any metaphysical doubt. My boldness, too, has its origin in this faith.[25]

This first context of being accepted is and remains for many people the most important source of faith and courage for living, and it is not difficult to see in the faces of the unhappy people who have never experienced any of this, what elementary injury their soul has sustained. And even when a woman may forget the infant at her breast — which does in fact happen among people — "yet I will not forget you", says God through Isaiah (Isa. 49:15).

These days, in the age of a complete radical change in our roles as women and men, such images are no longer as unambiguous as they once were, and I would be the last person who wants to go in for the mystique of motherhood, or to lay myself open to the suspicion of wanting to reverse the fact that Christians are breaking away from their medieval dependence and immaturity. What I should like to bring to mind is that with the total loss of such symbolic language our theology and our spirituality have lost that essential dimension of human existence and experience of God — the dimension generally referred to as the female. And so, unfortunately, we are still a church of fathers and brethren.

But there is yet another dimension to the image of the church as a mother, a dimension which it would be salutary for us to discover and practise for the benefit of our church and spiritual life. "Mother" cannot, after all, simply mean giving love; she is not just refuge and provider, she is also the one who conceives and gives birth. Conception and birth of what? Of the truth of Jesus. Is not generally the image that reflects our church that of one who has and knows it all, much more than that of one who conceives/receives? The administration of salvation is dominant over conceiving and bringing truth to birth. Are we so much in possession of the truth — the truth of the Reformation, for instance — that we are no longer capable of receiving/conceiving new forms of truth, such as liberation theology, feminist theology, black theology? How can we, from being possessors, become receivers? Do we practise such an attitude in our prayers and hymns? Can we ourselves, as a church, newly receive this truth, willing again and again to become fruitful? Are our church structures, is our thinking open to this? The church as the one who gives birth — such an image can help us to see all our great pain, fears and doubts in the daily work of the church as part of great ongoing birthpangs, through which the church is continually trying in new ways to bring the truth of Jesus to light in the world. The hard work in our synods and congregations, the struggles and fights must not be rejected as something fruitless. Bringing the truth of Jesus newly to light is, as with any birth, accompanied by labour, pain and mortal danger. There are no such things as cheap birth, prayer-wheel births; only labour, willingness, even offering up life itself, even the life of the church itself, maybe its close relationship with the state — for the sake of the truth.

The church I dream of is one where the truth of Jesus can grow afresh, again and again, a church that will not shy away from losing blood, power and life, in order that its precious knowledge may, ever new and fresh, enter into the world. I long for a church in which order does not have priority over growth; where tiny roots of love-of-the-truth are capable of breaking through the asphalt of dogmatism, covering it with its reconciling green; where struggle and pain are recognized not as an intrusive disturbance but as part of the process that leads to the discovery of the truth; where the new life in women's groups, peace groups, action groups is not put into a straitjacket, but where even uncontrolled growth is given space as part of the church's self-understanding — yes, is understood as scope for renewal. That is why our churches must be places where, through the blessing of divine seed received in our hearts, the incarnation of human beings can take place, where they are born again to be new, truly human, human-beings, who can lay aside that old human nature of the warmongers, the haters of strangers, the amassers of wealth, the home-and-garden fanatics, the anti-communists, the know-alls and the slanderers, in order to become new men and women who will not live at the expense of others, whether here or in the third world, but who will know that God's shalom is the kind of peace that does not tolerate people's injustice against people.

But all these things should not be "cerebral births"; they should take down-to-earth shape in life itself. In our churches, justice is more talked about than put into practice — fear, maybe, of justification by works? Bonhoeffer longed for the church to be a place for "prayer and righteous action". [26] That is what I yearn for, too. It seems as if we do not succeed in keeping these two things together in our churches. We simply must not allow our churches to degenerate into Jesus fan-clubs, where the idol is feted, but where no commitment is expected. If the church wants to avoid being a fan-club, or having its truth arise from "cerebral birth", then "prayer and righteous action" must be made to inter-relate in new ways.

Eberhard Bethge once interpreted this Bonhoeffer phrase beautifully:

> Righteous action among the people saves prayer from becoming an escape into self-satisfied piety. Prayer saves righteous action among the people from self-righteousness. Righteous action saves prayer from the hypocrisy among the pious which the children of this world will never fail to spot. Prayer saves righteous action from the fanatical ideologizing through which those who are committed to change become bad representatives of their own commitment. Righteous action saves prayer from pessimism. Prayer saves righteous action from resignation. Action keeps prayer in the realm of reality; prayer keeps action within the realm of truth. [27]

The church I dream of is a place where we can pray in reality, where we can develop a new spirituality which does not divide our body from our soul, where the gospel preached with "pure reason" is carried by a strong holistic piety; where we are concerned about people and the world, rather than about the salvation of our own souls; where calling someone a "starry-eyed idealist" has no cynical connotations; where the *praxis pietatis* comes right at the top of our agendas; where the fear of change is overcome by the joy about a new pluriform life; where the experience of the worldwide body of Christ is not only part of our own blood stream but raises us to new life — do we not experience this in a variety of ways?

Many wishes and dreams about the church. High expectations. To keep all this in perspective, I sometimes say a prayer by Bishop Colin Winter of Namibia:

God, remind me,
in case it is necessary,
that you have not commanded us
to defend your church, but to surrender our life
for the people. [28]

This is my constant inward and outward dialogue with the church, my declaration of love, translated into the poetry of the following lines:

Mother —
said the fathers traditionally
to the church.
She was like a mother to them
in the past.

She was like a father strict with me.
I soon forgot how to giggle and skip.
Law and gospel curbed my spirit —
strongly dualistic,
to tame the urge to improve the world,
while grace
was disembodied, soul-bound.
And I was left, disturbed, to ask:
Pious church, how about the world?
Are you selling her down the river
for a hereafter?

Yet at the same time there grew and lives
within your womb the fruit
whose weight of ages
wears and bears you out:
the irresistible, unarmed
truth of Jesus.
God so loved the world.

She prepares for herself
clear, unambiguous paths,
grows breaking through dogmatic asphalt,
jumps over ambiguous words,
becomes body and life.

Bread is baked for the hungry,
the tearful with their burnt-out hearts
now laugh.
In dead eyes hope awakes.
The rich young men begin to give their all
to the poor.
People hunger and thirst for
better justice than the present one
(not to speak of the ploughshares
that will take the place
of cruise missiles.)

Richly flows the water
of the Holy Spirit
through dried-out pews
out into the street where thirsty people sit.

Made strong, they pause and rise
to join God's protest movement
for the world,
that will not remain confused, irreconciled.

Today, said Kierkegaard,
we must again
bring Christ back into the church...

I have loved you since long and,
to my own delight,
will call you mother,
be nourished in your womb,
you, called to bring to birth the truth,
church.

The love you seek to bring to bear
embraces you,
and sets you free,
to become what you are:
not a club for smitten Jesus fans,
but a place for prayer
and righteous action.

3. Where do the dead go?

Letter to a child

My dear little girl,

Something dreadful has happened: while you were happily on holiday, your father died suddenly. His heart would not go on beating, although it was still a young heart. And so, very quickly and without saying much, he passed away, in the night.

It is something terribly hard for a child not to have a father any more. That is why I am writing this letter. Maybe it will help you a little, while you have so many questions, and your heart aches with homesickness for your father. I should like to tell you a little bit about him.

We first met years ago before ever you came into the world. Your father was a doctor in a children's hospital. I believe it was very important for him to spend his life caring for little children; he remembered from his own childhood how much fear and hurt children have to go through. Children are so much more vulnerable and helpless than grown-ups. That is why he worked for children when they were ill in body and in soul.

That was how I came to know your father. At the time I was with my little boy in the hospital where your father worked. Maybe you remember photographs of little Micha who spent nearly two years of his brief life in hospital, in a plastic tent. Like his little brother before him, Micha too had an incurable disease because of which his body was unable to resist any infection.

All that time your father and other doctors with him fought to keep little Micha alive. It was during that time that your father and I got to know each other well. We talked a lot together, especially about why children had to suffer so much, and about how one can help them. We used to think about what is going on in the minds of parents whose children are ill, and why life is so often like a big black sack people have to lug around with them.

At that time, I had to learn the worst, just as you have to now: that it is impossible to possess someone for ever. Each person has his or her own span of life. We enter life and leave it again according to God's will — whether it be short or long, whether it be beautiful or painful. You were born when my child was exactly one year old. Your parents sometimes brought you into the clinic when you were a baby, to visit Micha. You were like a little princess who wanted to visit the little prince in his enchanted plastic palace. You knocked on the palace gate, but were unable to enter. Micha would see you and laugh with you — a little enchanted prince, but no one was able to break the spell of that enchantment. You then became my godchild; ever since then you have been a little bit *my* child — in the same way that your parents wanted to have Micha as one of their own children. They shared with us in our suffering when he was too tired to go on living in his plastic castle, and left this earthly life. And now your daddy has also gone. Sometimes, you know, it was also difficult to find the way into the castle of your father's life, wasn't it? When Micha died, your mother wrote: "We have lost a child." The same is true today: we have all lost your daddy. Once we have laid him into the earth, the question that will stay with us is: Where is your daddy, where are Micha and Frieder, where is your grand-dad whose death you have also experienced? Where have they all gone?

I have thought a great deal about these things because I, too, wanted to know at the time what had happened to my children, where they are, how they are. In the same way you will want to know what has happened to your daddy. Yes, I know you are already very clever and you know lots of things, what it is like when someone dies. But how much do we really know about those who die? I believe that you as a child are among the first to whom I can explain what I discovered.

One thing is clear, and it is very painful: you cannot talk with the dead any more; you cannot laugh with them any longer, or eat with them. You cannot go for a walk with them or sleep by their side any longer. They cannot give you pleasure any more, or tell you off, or read stories to you, or help you with your homework or play with you. You cannot give them presents any more or receive any from them. You cannot go on a car journey with them, phone them or go on holiday with them. All that — and much more — is no longer possible.

They have gone away into another, invisible country — to a place where there are already many others: your grandfather, Micha and Frieder, and many other people are already there, ready to welcome your daddy. There are animals too, and plants. All of them, like all of us, will one day return to mother earth, who will receive us into her cool brown lap, and will put her earthly arms around us and give us a new home. The dead return to the place from which all life comes in the first place, to God who is there is the depth of the earth, in the heavens above, in people's hearts, everywhere.

God has a large soft lap — the Bible talks about Abraham's lap, but maybe you would rather think of your mother's lap. All those who once lived will find a place there, and God listens to them as they tell their earthly stories: about their troubles and joys, about the things that made them laugh and cry, about the people they used to live with, about you and me. God will laugh and be pleased, or will cry and be angry and indignant, all according to what they tell.

Isn't it lovely to imagine how your daddy and Micha are meeting each other, are thinking about the time when we were still all together at the hospital? After all, we had often been cheerful and happy there, when things used to go a little better for us all. We do not have much precise knowledge about the dead and so we have to make do with pictures like these, but they are true! There is one thing, however, which we know very clearly — and I have often seen it myself in their faces: the dead have entered into a great peace. Whatever may have tormented them or made them unhappy — worries, anger, struggle — it has all been taken away from them and they have come to rest. You have to look long and hard at dead people in order to discover this. It is frightening only if you just glance at them briefly.

We cannot live with them any longer. But we can go on loving them. They are still with us and they protect us. They help us in an invisible way. We can call out to them whenever we are talking about them with others. We can bring to life all the beautiful memories and have silent conversations with them. We can try to work out what they would say or do. We can look at pictures, or pick up things that used to belong to them. But the best thing of all is that we ourselves can, so to speak, carry on living a part of their life: they live in our hearts. The dead have a new home inside us, they are not lost.

It may well happen to you that you will be angry and furious about your daddy no longer being there, and so you should and may, because it would be expecting too much of a little girl — or of anyone for that matter — that she should simply accept what has happened.

One thing is certain, though: whatever heavy burden your daddy had to bear has now been lifted from him.

All of us who knew him are thinking with love and gratitude of what he was able to give us, of his serious and intelligent eyes, of his friendly laughter from under his moustache, of his beautiful hands with which he used to help children. I see him in front of me now on a photo I once took: you are still a very little girl and he is carrying you while you are clutching his finger — you look so tiny compared with him. He is laughing deep inside himself and he is happy.

Although you are still a little girl, you are not that small any longer because you have already learnt a great deal about life — more than some grown-ups; you have already learnt about death. When people have learnt from life as much as you already have, then it is possible for them to open their heart to the life of others around them. They notice more quickly when others are unhappy; they are able to understand them better, and to help them when help is needed. It is then a great source of joy to do all these things. At this time, you and your mother, your brother and the others, need such people around you who can give you much love, so that it may be a little easier for you to cope with the fact that your father has gone. I believe that God turns especially to the people who are having a hard time, in order to wipe away their tears. It isn't as if God takes the burden away, but God sends us people who carry us as Saint Christopher once carried the child Jesus, or he gives us strength in other ways to cope with our sadness, even when sometimes we would want to scream. I want to try and help you, share in bearing you up. In the in-between time God protects all the dead with great love and friendliness, not holding anything against them, no, not one little bit. The beauty of what was there between daddy and yourself, and all of us, will never be lost. In a completely different way, your daddy is very much alive and will always remain so in our hearts.

Which is why I embrace you with great love.

Your godmother

On the death of my child

Through the incision
in my flesh
you were cast
into the world.

Already,
while soft down
still clung
to your eyelashes,

your death
announced itself
in the test-tubes
in the laboratory,

death allowing you
time to focus
your big eyes
on us,
eager to live,
in searing pain,

so that a trace of eternity
might remain
in our lives.

4. To the "Theas" in a theologians' church

Bad marks for history up-to-now

There is an ever-growing number of "Theas" * about, women doing theology or working as ministers. They are close to my heart, because I know from experience something of what they are going through — things good and bad. I do not want to burden them with expectations, but they are to my mind a major source of hope for the church's future. If the church does not find a rightful place for the Theas, she will lose her last resource of strength altogether: the women. A straightforward prognosis. Therefore, all you women, you can take comfort: the church needs you! You are the blood transfusion a worn-out body needs, though maybe the body itself does not realize it yet.

True, not all Theas put the feminist challenge to the church, but those who do belong to the best and most committed in our universities and our congregations. The feminist challenge raises its head all over the place; it is in the very best sense a people's movement among the people of God, and it incorporates within itself women of completely different types and backgrounds. The Theas are only a small proportion of that. They belong to that larger women's movement in Christian churches all over the world, which embraces lay women and women theologians without hierarchical paraphernalia.

I am reading the minutes of a discussion among Theas about their studies and about their future in the church. I am disquieted by what they say. "The women are given a new place at the children's table," said one of them in a tone of resignation. "We have a women's church dominated by men," said another one. "I am living like a complete schizophrenic. On the one hand I have to absorb all the traditional curriculum stuff in which I myself do not feature; on the other hand I know that my feminist theology in which I do feature is not wanted and that in fact it will probably foul up my chances of future employment." One woman student had preached a trial sermon about Mary and Martha. The assessor gave her low marks on the ground that the sermon had no message for him as a man. Another high-up cleric, brought in as a consultant, came with the balanced argument that sermons should, after all, appeal to everybody.

---

* See translator's note in the preface.

What should women say about 2000 years of men's sermons, other than: "We cannot go on like this. Your exclusiveness, your sermons, your way of being-the-church, does not mean anything to us women any more; it certainly does not mean enough." Women still do not have the power to mark the examination papers of the men's church and write "failed" across them. But unfortunately, as so often, people vote with their feet. Many, far too many, are leaving to go into no-body's-land, the land of the goddess, because it is better than the desert where they are thirsty and hungry. The faithful have found a different way. When women's hearts have been hanging long enough in the chimney of male comfort, they have become sufficiently preserved and tough to survive a few years or centuries of winter. But now the women's spring has arrived. New blood throbs through the veins, desiring nothing less than lively people and lively women, a lively spirituality and church. The piety of grim endurance is over, once and for all.

The awakening of the women's movement in the church is a total Copernican change, both in breadth and in character. It calls into question the whole dominating male way of thinking, as well as the conception of the world moulded by men over the centuries. Who could possibly deny that the world has so far been interpreted by men? According to the story of the creation, Adam was given the privilege of naming all the animals, "and whatever he called each living creature, that was its name". (Gen. 2:19,20). Naming and interpreting the world is in tune with the masculine view of life. But it would be an illusion to think that seeing life from a male point of view equals seeing it from a human point of view. This world, as named and interpreted by the male half of the human race, is passed off as an objective and standard perception of the world. A professor recently rejected the work of a woman student on a feminist topic by arguing that it was too subjective.

A human being is a human being because he/she thinks; *cogito, ergo sum*, said Descartes, the man. Not because maybe he or she loves or acts or participates, or makes mistakes, or laughs or whatever else makes us human. The Cartesian think-person became a kind of leit-motif of theology — to its detriment. Piety came to be reduced to knowing what is theologically correct. Knowing and repeating the right formulae and creeds took the place of being integrally pious with mind, heart, mouth and hands! Descartes destroyed this wholeness not only in the field of theology, but also in medicine, physics, philosophy. The question about the *concept* of God replaced more and more the *experience* of God. Descartes and his followers really dug the grave for our ability to experience God.

When Copernicus first maintained that the earth was not the centre of the universe, but that it circled around the sun — and not the other way round — a complete world-concept (that of Ptolemy) collapsed. And the Bible and its expositors were deeply affected by it, because they had proclaimed everywhere their faith in the terminology of the Ptolemaic world-view. Till this very day, the fuss over this loss has not quite subsided.

The twentieth-century women's movement claims that the world and the faith do not circle around a male top-heavy axis, but that they also have a female pole which causes a different kind of vibration in the world: the Cartesian world-view collapses. And the Bible and its expositors are most deeply affected by it, because they were proclaiming the faith in the language of patriarchy. People are only just beginning to get excited about it, but the censors are already on the scene, crying out: we can't have that! "This is where the boundaries of legitimate theology are being crossed," it says in a position paper on feminist theology. [29] We shall have to start afresh jointly to negotiate as to who has the right — and when — to decide what is legitimate in those matters and what is not. When in their own interest churchmen make judgments on our theology, women plead bias. We women should really be allowed to discover a thing or two for ourselves and to make a few mistakes. If they label our discoveries as heresy, that is their problem. The men's church will have to clean up their own affairs; they will have their hands full after 2000 years! Hanging on to patriarchy would be like trying to reintroduce the Ptolemaic view of the world. Surely, the church would not want that. And the thing about heretics has always been that they have been banned and burned for what turned out to be right the day after tomorrow. They exercise an obedience that is running ahead, as it were.

Has the Bible then become useless because it employs the language of the Ptolemaic world-view? Has its truth about humanity and God been spoiled for the people today by wrapping it up in this way — as some have claimed? Not at all! We have seen through the wrappings; they belong to a particular time, and we have been rewarded by reaching more profound insights into the faith. Will the Bible become useless because it speaks a patriarchal language? Has its truth about God and humanity been spoiled for the people of today, for women, by wrapping it up in this way?

This is the thing on which our thoughts as Theas, as women engaged in feminist theology, are concentrated. A major factor in the exploration of this issue is going to be the way in which the men's church will come to grips with this challenge.

Singing the "Lord's" song in a strange land?

"I read my tradition with a loving heart and critical eyes." I learnt this beautiful phrase from the feminist Blu Greenberg, an orthodox Jew. I want to try and explain why I still love my tradition, yes, why I have only come to love it properly after my years of ecumenical wanderings. I do not love it because of its patriarchal form, but in spite of it all! Many Theas go through this patriarchal wilderness without much hope of ever conquering it. The church's patriarchy, and her character which is so much ruled, occupied and defined by men and by male committees, that fraternal company — "brotherland" — in which all (women included) have to be "brethren" because that happens to be the all-embracing definition of humanity; all that lies before us like an open book, and we are caught up in the painstaking and detailed job of deciphering the manifold manifestations of male supremacy and female subjugation.

Five years' work in male committees of the world church, of the oikoumene, with metropolitans, archbishops, bishops, presidents, churchmen in all shapes and sizes, have really opened my eyes to the extent to which sexism holds sway in the churches, and I must admit that as a result I tend to be more radical than ever. At the same time, however, I have also experienced that the courageous and frank confrontation by women has made it possible to break through the system, to gain ground and to make visible progress. Through intelligent, organized and concerted action by women, and with the support of some committed male feminists in the decision-making structures, we have had some success.

But how did we all get so stuck in that "brotherland" in the
first place? And, what is more: how are we going to get out of it
again, without leaving it to the "brethren"? Several women, in
their frustration, have tried to do it in this way; but that would
hardly be a new departure.

Aggressiveness in the feminist movement is, like everywhere
else where aggressiveness rears its head, a sign that there is an
imperviousness about. When the possibilities of change and of
bringing things out into the open are totally missing, the
potential anger and frustration among women will grow. The
"brotherland" seems to be so cussedly impervious to the questions of the women, that it gives rise to yet more aggression both
on the side of the women and on the side of the men's church, so
that it comes to ever more serious blows. Meanwhile, the
emigration of women continues apace. For how, they ask, can
they "sing the Lord's song in a strange land"? The sisters of
"Sweet Honey in the Rock", who will accompany us throughout
this book, are singing this famous gospel for the women who
have to live in a male-defined culture, and who do not know
whether they want to sing at all, least of all "the Lord's song".
The women sit by the rivers of Babylon, displaced, estranged,
full of homesickness, having hung their harps on the willows,
having been silenced for centuries (Ps. 137). No one took notice
of the language of their silence; not even they themselves; for
women it had become second nature to be silent, a second self...
They were silent into themselves, with their anger, their suffering, their inspiration, their knowledge, their joys. Reduced to
inner silence, women made out of this suppressed potential
small trivial things, which were "permitted". And so they
decorated homes, hats and altars. Or they nattered away in trite
conversation. They shed tears on their master's doormat, when
he had chosen someone else for the night, and they gave birth to
the next generation, delivering it into the hands of the same fate;
they were pleased with highly-priced sons, but were embarras-
sed over less-valued daughters, and were thrown out when
childless. The blame always fell on them. Or they went out of
their mind when the Faustian man, having enjoyed her virginity
and made her pregnant, went off in quest of higher things. He is
let off the hook; she pays with her life. Inside many of them
there continued to live an irresistible yearning for the female

half of God, and a secret conviction that there exists or existed something else. Kneeling in the pews, they brought their pious hearts, while at the same time they bore within them that banned self, sobbing with their longings, with a living body and a thinking head. They offered it all up, as commanded, to man, children, fatherland or some other noble purpose and finally — how crazy! — they offered it even to God. Women, submission is your name!

But there were always a few courageous women who were able to steal the knowledge man had withheld from them: writing and reading, studying, and they used it with audacity to share their experiences as did the mystics of the Middle Ages, whose God-centred knowledge is full of love and depth and female strength.

But there were also the others, the rebels, who were still conscious of the land of the great mother, or of the unadulterated moon, who regulates the inner life-clock, the woman's cycle, by her own rythm. With the moon, the days of fertility come and go like ebb and flow, blood and life. Women spend long periods of their life listening in to their bodies, whether new life is beginning to stir. How could they have forgotten the moon, seeing she keeps coming and going in a woman's life? Or mother earth, who bears her fruit in due season? But what was the very strength of the women came in "brotherland" under the verdict: dangerous! unclean! The great name-inventors changed it into shame and disgrace. But those who refused to bow down to this verdict, passed it on: this secret knowledge, in which for thousands of years no writer has been interested. They entrusted it to each other in whispers, at night and in the fog; whispered, hidden under their skirts: the knowledge of the wise women. But "brotherland" spoke its merciless "No". Great and little popes damned, abused, persecuted them and invented the name that would fit them: they were turned into witches because they refused to betray their gut feeling, their hunches. They tortured them because of their secret knowledge. They wanted to drag it out of them, beat it out of them with whips and tongs, on the rack and in the stocks, and then, finally — whether they had confessed or not — to burn them at the stake, to behead them, to drown them. You can read it all up in the witch-hunt records, the torture and the perfidious methods. One henchman boldly said: "If God did not want them to burn, he would have prevented it." That is what I call henchman-theology.

This is a piece of historical writing which the women of today are producing as seen from down below. Has it ever occurred to the church to come up with a confession of guilt or with reparation? They want to talk the women into reconciliation without repentance, partnership without equality. We are not calling for apologies on their knees, but after such a horror story, restraint in pronouncing judgments would at least be a sign.

But the story is not over yet. The proclamation of the progressive spirit of Reformation and Enlightenment was not allowed to pass the women by. Mrs Käthe (Luther) was given her role to play: the Protestant minister's wife was born. Later, they finally succeeded in extending the priesthood of all believers so as to include the women. Please note, though; at the price fixed by the men's church. In "brotherland" they think differently, pray differently, they have different priorities, they laugh about different things. What follows is the — typical? — story of a woman on her way into the men's church:

While she was still in the girls' club or at worship, she had not yet noticed anything.

It all started during her theological studies, when she discovered that at no point was there a woman at the centre of academic attention. Only by going out and looking for herself did she meet Hildegard von Bingen, the prophetic mystic, and Elisabeth von Thuringen, who gave all she had to the poor, and also the courageous Joan of Orleans whom they burned at the stake. There were very few examples of independent women from whom she could have taken her cue. She assumed the expected male manners. She learnt not to talk about personal things, not to take women seriously any longer (with the exception of mothers, of course), to model her thinking and behaviour on the careers and thoughts of famous men. She learnt how to be cool and clear in analyzing issues scientifically and to come to well-balanced choices. Never in her life had she seen a woman minister in the pulpit until she herself entered it for the first time. More and more she adapted herself to the male culture, accepted the style of the men's organizations in which she had to function. There they have their own regulations, rituals, manners of speech and thought, ways-of-doing-things, relationships among themselves. They have their own ways of exercising power, hiding aggressions behind questions about points of order and behind brilliant formulations. And so she has had to try and prove that she, too, could do all these things.

It was only the "brethren" who featured in the language of the order of service, the verses of the hymns and in many Bible passages. Women's problems, the joys and pains of loving, sexuality, marriage, having children, contraception, death, separation, body, feelings, but also questions of justice generally, and justice for women — all these were largely alien for "brotherland". They did not fit into its well-ordered framework — in the area of civil service legislation within the church, for instance. Was she mistaken or not in thinking that the gospel had something to say to these questions? It was only gradually that she gained the confidence to voice these questions, encouraged by feminist literature and conversations with women about this matter. A patronizing openness permitted her to bring a quality of human warmth to bear on the sober order of business — through songs, flowers, pictures, small variations in style, through creating a little space for the personal. But she kept asking herself whether this was really all. Was this really all Jesus had in mind when he called people to discipleship? Were the first Christian congregations not chiefly made up of women and slaves? The question remains valid: How can she as a woman sing God's song in the 'brotherland' church? She did not just want to sing about the obvious, the expected, but her own Song of Zion. She did *not* want to hang her harp on the willows and keep silence — not again.

What I have described here is the stance of many Theas today who reach this point with all its possibilities much earlier in life than I did. Because the example given above is my own story.

Provocation

Feminist theology has unmasked the sexist structures of church language, theology and social policies. It is fundamentally challenging the church to recognize the distortion of the Christian message created by the church's patriarchal socialization, and to reconstruct its social patterns, language and theology to affirm the full humanity of both women and men. [30]   This is how Rosemary Radford Ruether describes the challenge of feminist theology. This critique is a pre-condition for the renewal of a church in which nobody will be diminished, or robbed of his or her God-given divine likeness, for reasons of sex, race or whatever other grounds there may be — overt or hidden.

Feminist theology, seen in this way, is hermeneutically the key issue for theology of the second half of the twentieth century, as part of the theology of liberation; and it should be taken as seriously as the dialectical theology of the first half of this century, and therefore it should not be ridiculed because it comes from women and speaks a different language.

The church has already had to grapple with many similar challenges. She has always put up a fight, as in the case of the abolition of slavery. But she has had to battle through — and it has never done her any harm. She merely became more honest as a result of it, and in the last resort we have to keep saying that it is God who preserves the church. The Copernican revolution, the Enlightenment, historical-critical science, demythologizing have all put the church to the test, but they have ultimately set her free to be her true self. This is why it is important for us women to articulate clearly what we have to say and ask. I should like to have a go at this.

Through historical-critical research we have learnt that the Bible did not neatly and tidily fall from heaven, but that it was written by many people, spread over the span of centuries. They wrote down their experiences of God in the languages and thought-patterns of their own time, the prophets, the priests, the tentmakers and many others. They wrote with the slate pencil of the history that was contemporary with such people as Nebuchadnezzar, Augustus, Cyrus and Herod. Everything that was handed down came through the prism of the human eye, of the human heart, of the human language, and tradition was therefore coloured humanly. Through this insight, biblical research has been enormously helped to come to a better and deeper understanding of the Bible with all its contradictions. Now today the women come with a new crucial hermeneutical discovery: the biblical scriptures, as far as we know, have all been written by men, which means that the message has come through yet another prism — that of a male experience of life — and has been coloured accordingly.

But there is more: the writers of the biblical sciptures lived in a patriarchal society where men mattered and counted; women and children did not. "Some five thousand men shared in this meal, to say nothing of women and children" (Matt. 14:21: the feeding of the five thousand).

Because of the way biblical passages came together, women's experiences of God were largely excluded, especially when one realizes that women had little or no access to scriptures and synagogue. Despite this, innumerable facts about the role of women in the life of Jesus and in the history of salvation have been preserved, as have a number of other fragments of matriarchal tradition. But during the subsequent centuries, women were virtually unable to bring their knowledge to bear on the way church history was shaped. "It has pleased God to reveal himself thus (Father, Son and Holy Spirit) and in no other way."[31] How in the world can it have pleased God that the most faithful witnesses of God's life and death were excluded from the shaping of tradition, because a male culture had banned them from public religious life? No, it is impossible that God was pleased with this pride of male tradition, which went so far as to turn the Trinity into a pure male threesomeness. Originally, in Hebrew, Spirit — *ruach* — is feminine; in Greek, Spirit — *pneuma* — is neuter; it isn't until you come to Latin that Spirit becomes masculine — *spiritus*; as is the case in German — *Geist*.

But the real provocation lies not so much in the fact that the tradition which was formed by men excluded women, as that it actively took a stance against women and against any remnants of matriarchal religion. The traces of the women's history in the early church became increasingly vague. Even Paul completely fails to mention the women as eye-witnesses of the Easter morning happening (1 Cor. 15:4-8). And so the women, as bearers of divine revelation, were more and more pushed to the periphery, and were not incorporated in the lectionaries which, after all, until the time of the Reformation, were for the faithful the only direct access to the Bible.

Selective reporting was introduced; the church mothers disappeared into the night of history. Soon these manipulated facts were elevated to be the accepted norm; it was accepted as normal that women (apart from the Virgin Mary) did not feature in the tradition, so that in the end no one asked any questions any more about the contribution which the women had made. It isn't until today that we are posing this question, and therefore it comes across as an enormous provocation, because it exposes the way in which masculine privileges and prejudices came to be interwoven with tradition.

Women in the feminist movement go so far as to identify in the Old Testament the deliberate campaign by paternal religion against the "queen of heaven", the goddess of fertility (Jer. 7:18). And many women no longer recognize the victory of the former over the latter as "good news". The symbols of women's religion, serpent and fertility, were given a negative meaning, or differently interpreted: the serpent, symbol of wisdom (as Jesus showed when he spoke of "being wise as serpents..."), becomes a temptress. Adam the man (with God's help) gave "birth" to Eve the woman from one of his ribs (like Zeus to Athena from his head), and consequently the myth of birth, that domain of woman, was expropriated and broken up.

But the patriarchal colouring of the tradition went even further. Men have the power to give names, to define, to legitimize, to decide (till this very day). That is how male and female sexuality — in all religions for that matter — came to be defined by men. Female body functions, like menstruation and birth, were declared "unclean", which then motivated the exclusion of women from the altar. Female sexuality became a threat to man's free will, which comes right at the top of the patriarchal scale of values. Man simply appears to be helpless before female sexuality, and his will seems unable to tame, control or wilfully stimulate sexual desire.

What a defeat for the male spirit which takes "being in control" so much for granted! Whatever sexuality may have meant to women themselves was irrelevant. Whoever wants to know this more precisely should read what Augustine has to say about the Fall. [32] That is how woman came to be called "evil temptress". Caught up in nets like that, women's identity and sexuality were diminished to the level that the patriarchy wanted and permitted: tamed, dependent beings, like pets, who, beyond the fulfilment of their duties as mothers and wives, had no further claims or ambitions.

All this may sound harsh, but the history behind it, and about which the women are raising their voices — often angry and shrill — is much harsher. If in the way I have expressed myself — I admit it — some things came across as coarse, remember that the denial, the silencing, the mal-formation of women is an equally coarse betrayal of God's plan that they should reflect the divine likeness, and that the reconciled community in Christ should fully include women and men.

Walking with un-bound feet

The Theas and many Christian women are today experiencing an elementary liberation event: it sounds as if it could come straight from the Bible, and so it does (Luke 13:10-13: the healing of the crippled woman). We have been wearing these little Chinese shoes far too long, but after having been bound up for centuries, our feet are being unwrapped. Among ourselves as sisters we carefully undo the bandages of our mal-formation — and the smallness and pitifulness of what is revealed is our female self, of which people generally, but also we ourselves, had been saying that it was beautiful the way it used to be. Little feet were all right for teetering, but they were too small for real footsteps, for stepping out independently. They were feet which always needed to be guided, always needed male support.

Now it hurts, it often hurts terribly, to feel the stress and strain, to feel the freedom of movement, which is a bit like being suddenly unprotected and therefore somewhat frightening. We stare at our mal-formation which is like an accusation against ourselves, and we cannot bear the sight: so much wasted life throughout the centuries! Sometimes we are tempted to put the old bandages back on, instead of bearing this strange new experience. But no, you Theas! We must learn to walk. Freedom is not always immediately beautiful. We must learn to live with the uncertainty of our un-bound feet, and to encourage others to put up with our staggering and our search for support. Don't let them tell you that our searching lacks structure and that our staggering means incompetence. After all, we are only just beginning, our feet are staggering around. Some are already more sure of themselves, some even jump ahead. They can see

which way they want to go; they have managed it. But let us not
leave behind us those who are only just beginning.

We must devote ourselves, again and again, to the process of
un-binding. The hesitation and the pains of our slower sisters
are something about which we should care deeply. And so I see
ourselves as a women's movement on the way. There are so
many who are searching, faltering, knocking themselves against
stumbling blocks, and who desperately want to know how they,
too, will be able to talk. No, we're not talking about marching,
nor processing, nor marking time — what we want is *walking*
with un-bound feet.

Among all the women who are slowly beginning to walk, in
the church as well as outside it, there are those who are drawn
down into ravines and valleys in order to rediscover the life-
rhythm of nature and of their own bodies, and newly to bring
back to life the forgotten female rites out of the cycle of dying
and rising. In order to gain strength in the struggle against the
ruthless machinery of meaninglessness which has severed body,
soul and spirit from us all, they come together in celebration.
They are hoping that after the strictness of a father-god they
will fare better under the all-loving mother-goddess. They are
hoping that she may be able to keep the earth from the abyss,
through her ever-returning healing power. There is much seri-
ousness, courage and honesty among them. Most of them have
come to the conclusion — unfortunately — that the Bible is
against them. Christian symbols are being replaced by fertility
symbols.

Then there are those others who want to stand in the tradition
of the Easter morning eye-witnesses and to link up with the
rekindled life which they found there. They have left the cross
behind them, not as a discarded, empty death-symbol which
must give way to something else, but because of their deep
experiences of the anguish which the blindness of the human
heart has caused to the One as well as to the many throughout
history. They follow in the footsteps of those women who on
that particular morning were persuaded that the life of Jesus,
and every life, is eternally indestructible — resurrection from
the cross and the tomb. They began to proclaim Easter, faith in
life itself and in the abolition of all crosses; for this cross of
Jesus was meant to be the last one on which one person was

made to die for the people; in other words, it was the end of human sacrifices. Alongside Deborah, Miriam, Mary and many others in the Bible, these women are singing a stirring song of God, who is on the side of the weak and sends the rich empty away (Luke 1:46-55: the Magnificat). They believe that the prophetic spirit of the Bible has not ceased to be at work — after all, it was poured out on sons *and* daughters (Acts 2:17,18) — but that it will free the church from her patriarchal inflexibility through the unpredictable way in which it will blow, whether softly or with consuming fire.

There are, however, many others who have difficulty in tuning in to these thoughts and spiritual problems, because the daily struggle for life and survival, against crosses and crucifixions, against death in all its varied forms, demands all the energy they can get. They strengthen themselves for this task through communal prayer and celebration, with bread and wine in remembrance of the death of Jesus, which could also be their fate whenever they put their life at risk for the sake of others, whenever they need to come face to face with the principalities and powers of this world. Among them, and even right in their vanguard, are women like Domitila de Chungara from the tin mines in Bolivia. She organized a hunger strike in the midst of starvation, in order to obtain better living conditions.[33] Or Rigoberta Menchu from Guatemala who has to experience how her people are being destroyed, and rises up against it.[34] Among them are also the women of the Plaza de Mayo in Argentina, who each Thursday for years now have been marching up and down in silent protest in front of the government palace in Buenos Aires, in order to obtain information about their disappeared children. And the Philippino nuns who are demonstrating their concern for the young prostitutes, and exposing the scandal of the human slave trade. Or the Babushkas in Russia who are keeping the church alive. The women in the peace movements and the anti-apartheid movements everywhere: they get to grips with these issues through practical action, for whatever the question about God-father or mother-goddess may be, the surest way of finding an answer lies in looking at the faces of the women, men and children who have been entrusted to us, and in whom God, as woman, man or child, meets us and waits for our response.

The fear inside the men's church ought not to surprise us, the age-old fear of losing control, of being confronted with their own repressed half of being-human. The discussion does in fact focus on substantial rather than on periphal issues (*adiaphora*). But was it not always the substance which was at the heart of things whenever basic questions about the meaning of life were being posed? After all, the irrelevant squabbles from the history of theology, which have often occupied us far too much, will soon be forgotten. Today it is we, the women, who have taken over the role of "complicating the history of salvation", as my friend Elsa puts it (see chapter 6). In all these things we are by no means the first to take action; we have our predecessors in the Bible.

For the history of salvation never unfolds along predictable lines; but makes its detours via the unexpected.

For the dialogue among the women

For the further dialogue among the feminist women, I should like to offer two thoughts I am dying to share.

It is to the women's movement that we owe the insight that patriarchal thinking is responsible for splitting the world up into dualisms: male-female; white-black; light-dark; thinking-feeling; word-deed; spirit-body; conscious-unconscious; amongst others.

Patriarchal thinking has not only placed these dualisms in opposition to each other, but also put a value on them; the former was always better than the latter. This way of thought has caused great damage to the world. We want to free ourselves from dualisms, recognizing that they have prevented us from seeing the world in proper perspective. This is why it is fundamentally important that we should revalue the hitherto devalued half, make it ascertainable, and practise it. Hence also the search for the female qualities of God. For just as human beings need a mature relationship both to father and mother, so in the experience of God we see the reflection of male and female traits in the anthropomorphic language that uses human images. But we ought not to get into a position where we have to make choices yet again. Please, not again one thing at the expense of something else. Not the female instead of the male.

That is a shadow of the old spirit, and I cannot see any way forward in it. After all, the world is not either white or black. The world is always both at the same time. Sometimes it is good, sometimes bad, and most times good and bad at the same time. We need to get away from dualism, but not through naming new scapegoats. Away with sin; the sinner may live!

The other thing is almost more important to me. I regret that in the Western women's world there is such an absence of dialogue with sisters around the world about these questions. We are stewing too much in our own juice. In all this, I am afraid, the feminist women do not really get a better write-up than their patriarchal brothers. The risk of social blindness is a danger that affects both women and men.

They appear to enrich the inner fire of our own soul and faith at the expense of discerning what is going on in the world.

It grieves me to hear women say: "Don't bother me with the third world. I need to find myself." Are these really matters that unfold one after the other? First clearing up one issue, and then going on to the next? As far as I am concerned, the more I went out into the world around me, to South Africa, to the third world, the more I found myself. It was there that my female self was wakened in a different way, but it was wakened. But I am aware that that is not everyone's way. I am also fond of joining my sisters in the round dance at feminist gatherings, and I love the silence in which the whole body is involved. Nevertheless, what I far too often miss in many women's books and meetings of women is the word justice. There is a kind of inwardness of a western landscape of the soul gleaming through, with which we have had an affair for a long time. I do not wish to be put before the alternatives: pious or social. It cannot be like that: first becoming clear within myself and only then going out — I do not believe it is as simple as that. It could well be that the ingredients of my self-knowledge are to be found outside myself.

Once the bread has been baked, it is too late to add the yeast. Once my spiritual self has been formed, it is often too late to incorporate justice in it. It is while the dough is being kneaded that everything has to go into it. Meditation, prayer, struggle all belong together, they do not neatly come one after the other.

What else are we meditating about anyway? The Bible says that Jesus opened people's eyes wherever they were. He opens people's eyes, so that they may all the more clearly see the world around them, so that it in turn may stir them inwardly, in their heart, and they will be able to shape something out of that for the future. So open your eyes, you Theas, you, sisters, and see what you have not yet seen before. Let it move within your hearts. This is the beginning of all knowledge of God.

We had better get used to the fact that we no longer have access to the alchemist's kitchens which in the Middle Ages used to produce their images of God; there are a few things which historically cannot be reversed. The gods which arise from human thinking, as Feuerbach declared, have been unmasked. We cannot newly invent anything any more; all we can do is find what is already there in the strata of history. What is lost, suppressed, we are able to find or put in its rightful place and perspective. But a return to the lost paradise of the great Mother-Goddess is not possible for us. The only direction open to us is forward, towards God's realm, where there will be no more suffering, no crying or pain of women or of anyone, and where God like a mother will wipe the tears from our eyes and live with us under one roof, close to us; for the old order has passed away (Rev. 21:3,4: God's dwelling among men — and women), the rule of patriarchy, any form of lord-ing it over others, will be broken; women, men and children will distribute bread and wine and milk and honey, and all of them shall be satisfied, because they have worked, prayed, suffered, thought and felt for the realm of God, with body and soul. A new heavens and a new earth, the home of justice for all people.

Dear Theas: one more word among ourselves. While it is true that in the Old Testament there is a drive for the abolition of the female fertility cult, I do think that there is another thing we have to tackle in the church today, and which is also in the Bible, namely the abolition of the male potency cult. When Paul abolished circumcision as an initiation rite into the religious community (Gal. 5:1-6), he did two things: first of all he opened up the new faith to the gentiles, women and men, in that he went beyond the narrow ethnic, racist understanding of election. In Christ there is neither Greek nor Jew. His vision was one of widening out, not narrowing down. Secondly — and for this we need feminist exegesis — he abolished a rite that venerated male fertility. There should be no doubt, in terms of comparative religion, that male circumcision as a rite of entry into the cultic community was in fact identical with a recognition and adoration of male fertility. (This is why they worship phallic symbols in so many religions.) Had this not been the case, they might perhaps just as well have pierced the ears of girls and boys or done something else. Paul has clearly abolished the act of giving prominence to male fertility as a rite of entry into the new faith. The church may have discontinued the ritual, but not her inner attitude towards it. Because the conduct of worship in the majority of cases has remained in male hands. As a matter of fact, I have always wondered why during our theological education no one has ever explained to us the deeper meaning of circumcision.

In the Christian congregation one is not received on the basis of one's maleness, but through baptism — women and men equally, through a cleansing bath by which human beings are born anew from water and the Spirit.

Baptism as re-birth — that does not sound so patriarchal any longer. So much for Paul's actions, who, by the way, cannot be held solely responsible for the fact that subsequent church fathers turned the Corinthians passage, "women should not address the congregations" (1 Cor. 14:33,34), and not the Galatians one, "in Christ there is no male and female" (Gal. 3:28), into the foundation on which they based their "treatment of women". What we could have done with were the voices of the Lydias and the Priscillas, the Loises and the Eunices, who according to Paul's own testimony were most certainly not silent in those early congregations.

Twelve theses for Theas

For my own benefit and for you, Theas, I have put together the following theses to stimulate further thinking, discussion and action.

1. The women have themselves begun to name the world afresh. The right to give names, to define, decide what is justifiable will from now on be measured by women and men on an equal footing. The men's church will have to get used

to feminine names and words. We will not let this right be taken away from us by them, nor will we uncritically bow to definitions handed down from the past.

2. The themes that affect us mentally, physically and spiritually are important. We will not be talked out of them. They are the testbed for all existential honesty.

3. We are the church as much as any others. We often lack this self-understanding. The church needs the gifts of all its members. Without our feminine-critical questions and contributions she will become all the poorer.

4. Our strength does not lie in numbers — although we are constantly growing — but in our determination and our powers of persuasion. We share in the responsibility for ensuring that the old mother church will yet bring a beautiful child into the world.

5. We want to look at tradition through the eyes of the kind of women that we are. We are looking for the lost coin in the history of the church and theology. They will not be able to blame us for not being well informed about the things of the past. It is there, after all, that questions of humanness used to be grappled with. We want newly to discover them behind their often sterile apparel. We must quite independently learn how to use the languages of the Bible. They are full of meaning, in ways about which the patriarchal biblical scholars did not have the slightest idea.

6. We shall have to reckon with the possibility of having to live in the women's diaspora for some time yet. But we will not allow ourselves to be forced into a ghetto. Let us therefore create opportunities for meeting as women, exchanging ideas, helping and strengthening each other. Let us organize ourselves. Let us expose the things that oppress us; let us voice appreciation where help is given.

7. Let us talk with the sisters who are already in the ministry. It is possible to learn from what they are trying to achieve. It is often quite amazing how much of human sharing can be promoted by a woman minister, especially among women who would never confide in a man with their female problems. Then there are the "faithful women of the church" among whom there are real treasures to be found, and who are able to give us much help. We shall have to struggle to

make sure that more and more women in the church will participate in decision-making, in local church councils, in synods, in committees, in national executive circles.

8. We want to create new models of exercising ministry, not hierarchical but open and accessible. There is no need for us to be pushed into roles we do not wish to play. It is important that we should be honest with ourselves and with others. The gospel is the salt of the earth; some will smart from it, and so will we ourselves. The word "well-balanced" is no biblical term.

9. Let us remain open in our relationship with the male leadership in the church; they, too, want and need something new. And they are more grateful for our courage than we think. Being able to differentiate is in this case a step forward.

10. When we are together we want to worship and celebrate with one another. New forms of liturgy and prayers, singing, dancing and acting will develop. There is enough that will need to be brought before God. Let our spirituality be down to earth and clearly focused. We must figure in it, but not remain the subject.

11. Dialogue and cooperation with other denominations is very important. How much do we know about the other religions, about dissidents, atheists, workers, the unemployed, outsiders, young people? Let us be ecumenical, worldwide. The church we are serving is only a province. There is a lot women can learn in the worldwide oikoumene.

12. Let us work towards a renewed community of women and men. Too often, the old patterns have become "old hat" indeed. We are looking for new opportunities to help women and men in the church to become human beings who will be more free, more alive, more exuberant. To achieve this, we shall not hesitate to swallow, as well as to mete out, harsh criticism; it will serve the process of renewal.

Through it all, we want to stick by the wisdom of Jesus when he gave us this piece of good advice: "Be wise as serpents, and innocent as doves" (Matt. 10:16).

5. The power of the footwashers

Women stepping out of the darkness of history

At the end of Bertolt Brecht's *Beggar's Opera* are the words: "For some are in darkness and others are in the light. And the ones in the light are visible, but the ones in the dark are not." We belong to a generation of women who are emerging from obscurity into the light of history. Women who, until now, featured only marginally or not at all in the writing of world or church history, are growing out of the narrow confines of family responsibility to which, willingly or unwillingly, they had been restricted. Women who, irrespective of their social position, have throughout the centuries been able only in exceptional cases or indirectly, under the ruse of weakness, to influence the powerful, are now playing a more direct part in shaping public life in the church and in society. On the tough road to equality we have met with a lot of humiliation, jealousy, self-doubt and weakness and it will be good for us to identify these experiences we have had on our journey from darkness into light, from powerlessness to power, and to discuss them with each other.

Do we really want power as it now exists and as we see it exercised by so many of those in authority in the church and in society? Should we not all rather be looking critically at power and searching for new ways of using it? What have all the experiences of powerlessness done to our lives as women? How shall we apply this vast store of experiences in powerlessness when as women we assume responsibility and power?

Does power change the person who wields it, does it change us, women, too — and if so, how? So many necessary questions to which there are no simple answers, but they must not detract from the fact that women today want to and ought to take on responsibility for all of life, courageously and readily. To them and myself I simply say: have courage!

I have been thinking particularly about how we as Christian women could handle the wish for more influence and power, for power and powerlessness do not operate in a vacuum. They are also connected with our faith. "Thine is the power", we pray in the Lord's prayer. What does a sentence like this mean in relation to our longing for power, to our use of power, to our powerlessness?

Power and powerlessness are not among the classical themes in theology. Is this purely accidental? In these times of confrontation between powers and super-powers which has brought the world to the brink of the abyss, we have to look penitently and self-critically at the biblical understanding of power and power-lessness and at the way in which we should bring it to bear with new force in the area of political decision-making. For the message of Jesus was not just meant for the private corners of the soul; it was intended for the whole person and for the whole world. I believe that at the present point in human history only radical alternatives can show the way out of the blind alleys into which church history and world history have led us. Could it be that we women who are "beginners" in the power game have an opportunity here to give a reminder of something that could be a possible alternative? Whatever the case, there is no smooth and direct path that will lead us straight to power, nor should there be.

Power and liking

In the dictionary of etymology I recently discovered that in German the words *Macht* (power) and *mögen* (to want, to like) are both derived from the same Old High German root *magan*. I have been playing around a little with these words and came up with the following:

Power and liking

Liking power
being able
having the means
without means
without power
powerlessness
God's power comes to its full strength
in weakness. (2 Cor. 12:9)

Nobody likes me
I do not like myself
you are im-possible
in-capable
powerless

I like you
God likes me
I like myself
liking the world
liking the enemy
full of possibilities
full of power
almighty
Everything is possible
to one who has faith. (Mark 9:23)

Thinking about the root meanings of these words makes it clear that power and liking, power and love are somehow related to each other. The origin of these words still shows us something of how people are enabled, empowered through love; the love of people, the love of God.

Wherever the connection between power and love is lost, or the one is no longer bound up with the other, power becomes something menacing and dangerous, it degenerates into domination and arbitrariness. Detached from the foundation which legitimizes, it becomes something which human beings usurp for themselves, enjoy and misuse. Power becomes self-sufficient, making powerless those over whom it is wielded. It was for the sake of power that the phrase of the end justifying the means was coined. Power often seeks to make and keep people dependent. It creates a distance between those who have power and those who have not. It surrounds itself with status symbols. It seeks to increase its means of control (knowledge, authority, money) rather than sharing them. All this can be found on a large scale in both state and church. Can we possibly break this dynamic of wielding power?

The church's longing for power
There is only a thin dividing line between assuming necessary authority and exercising power in a negative sense. The urge to wield power and authority clad in the robes of the church, to win power over the souls and minds of the faithful, to exercise authority over subordinates and property has always been strong. The attraction of relating to each other as sisters and brothers, the community of mutual help and of sharing in the

search for truth have time and time again been undermined by this lust for power.

When, under Constantine, the early church became the official church of the Roman state, she put the gospel at stake for the sake of power. Her message of humility and poverty did not change the power of the state; what changed was the church herself.

She deluded herself with the hope that the influence she gained would make her better able to serve the gospel. But she failed to notice how the content of the message — rejection of violence, attachment to poverty and love of one's neighbour, the humility of service — was being eroded until it survived only among some marginal groups. All that remained were the empty husks of Christian language to dress up what were in fact secular forms of power. Christian Western rule blossomed magnificently. The name of Christ was used to legitimize all manner of power. Under the sign of the cross empires were founded, thrones established, crowns fashioned, wars waged, minds enslaved. This pattern has continued over the centuries.

Today, the content of the Christian message is again being sacrificed, this time under the guise of defending religious freedom: on the pretext of Christian anti-communism the people of our countries are being educated to fear the enemy and support political intransigence. The whole of God's creation is being placed at risk in the name of maintaining a so-called free market economy which is incapable of solving the problem of hunger in the world. Nuclear missiles are being produced at the expense of the world's poor. In the USA, a nuclear submarine which carries with it millionfold annihilation bears the name "Corpus Christi". People in Latin America, South Africa, the Philippines (under Marcos) and elsewhere are being tortured and killed by regimes which seek to give an air of respectability to their use of violence by adding the label "Christian".

And what of my church in the Federal Republic of Germany? Are we not bound by far too many political loyalties, privileges and compromises, to a middle-class culture and the political establishment? What do we sacrifice for God's sake so that the gospel can have the advantages and financial security of a

"Volkskirche", a state-dependent church? Love of power, yearning for power are behind much of this.

Those who assume responsibility are inevitably walking on a knife-edge between service and exercising power. How can we stay closer to the forces that can correct us, and protect us from the love of power?

Majesty and the washing of feet

Matthew tells us how Satan tempted Jesus with worldly power and splendour (4:8-10). Christ resisted this most basic of human temptations. In our theological education and in our churches we have always tended to gloss over this story much too quickly. Jesus' answer to Satan is: "You shall do homage to the Lord your God and worship him alone." God is the critical point of reference in all use of power. Not just any god, but the God who is love and to whom Jesus binds himself in service. And it is simply not possible to do just anything in God's name. So how is it that again and again in the church we find authoritarianism under the misnomer of "service"? How can it be brought to unmask itself; how can we unmask it?

The people in the Old Testament who in the second commandment were told not to make images of God nonetheless often imagined God as a mighty king, richer, mightier and more powerful than all earthly kings, though admittedly a king of justice and peace. This motif has been given form in countless works of art and music. The projection of images of monarchical power on to our ideas of God has induced the earthly "representatives of Christ" — popes, patriarchs, bishops, priests — to surround themselves with the insignia of a monarch's power and splendour — robes, titles, crowns, servants and official cars.

The Reformation notwithstanding, Protestant ministers and dignitaries, too, are not averse to surrounding themselves with an aura of unapproachable dignity and importance.

Jesus did not see his mission in terms of spreading royal power. The fact that his kingdom is not of this world has to mean that it is not made of the same stuff as the empires the powerful build for themselves. He put on an apron and washed his friends' feet. In his *Letters and Papers from Prison*, Dietrich Bonhoeffer wrote on this subject:

> Who is God? Not in the first place an abstract belief in God, in his omnipotence etc... Encounter with Jesus Christ. The experience that a transformation of all human life is given in the fact that "Jesus is there only for others"... Faith is participation in this being of Jesus... The church is the church only when it exists for others. To make a start, it should give away all its property to those in need... (it) must share in the secular problems of ordinary human life, not dominating, but helping and serving. [35]

Jesus did not come to serve here in our earthly world in order to reign all the more powerfully in another world beyond. His answer to the disciples whose thoughts were on power and on who among them would be greatest in the kingdom of God was: You have understood nothing at all. A king's first duty is to serve, and to do so always and everywhere: "You know that in the world rulers lord it over their subjects, and their great men make them feel the weight of authority; but it shall not be so with you. Among you, whoever wants to be great must be your servant, and whoever wants to be first must be the willing slave of all — like the Son of Man; he did not come to be served, but to serve..." (Matt. 20:25-28). And a disciple of Christ remains a servant, he or she does not become a cabinet minister in the kingdom of God. It is the children and the meek who inherit the kingdom.

The New Testament tells us that it was clearly the women around Jesus who were the first to understand the essence of his message correctly. Could this be because they had long been familiar with serving? Long after the rank-conscious disciples had left the scene, disappointed and disillusioned, the women were still there at the foot of the cross. They had come to believe that the power of selfless love, brought into the world and lived out by Jesus, cannot be overcome by any other power — not even by the power of death. That was their Easter witness. They were the first witnesses to this truth. They even told it to the disciples, who did not believe them (Luke 24:11).

Jesus confronted the love of power with the power of love. He did not just point to the kingdom of God, he also demonstrated in his own life the steps which lead to it. At every step along the way the goal must remain visible; if at any stage it does not, then that step is a false step. This is why, for example, God's power is to be found today wherever a mother teaches her child to pray and instils in its heart respect for God and humankind, wherever a young man in an African village digs a well or washes an old person instead of pointing a gun at other human beings. God's power is also to be seen among the powerless people who fight against nuclear weapons by distributing pamphlets, mere sheets of paper against the vehicles of death.

The irresistible power of truth and love — that is God's power. It has to do with solidarity, compassion, sharing, not deterrence and the defence of accumulated consumer goods.

The community of footwashers

Should we women today, ready at last to take our share of responsibility in power, simply forget this truth?

Christian patriarchs throughout the ages have certainly pre-scribed obedience and service as the appropriate role for women, while Germany's national poet, Schiller, wrote: "Let women early learn to serve and rule through serving." This does not, of course, mean the division of labour in which the service of women is essential so that the men can "serve" in high positions. The interpretation of the Bible by which the "servants of the word" came to identify obedience and humility as a woman's first duty, thereby creating the image of the woman as compliant servant, was a dishonest interpretation. Submissive-ness and immaturity, not having an opinion of their own, nor trying to shape their own lives, have all too often been the ingredients of this imposed servanthood, this "Christian" ideal of womanhood. It is only service rendered willingly and responsibly, not submissively and by imposition, which is and always will be a hallmark of true Christian discipleship. Perhaps the task that lies ahead for us women is to work at dismantling the hierarchies and privileges which prevent us in our churches from "washing one another's feet". It could be our specific contribution as women who are ready to assume responsibility and power, that we, with more determination than before, should devote our imagination, energy and time to building a "community of footwashers". This means we cannot continue to go along with the existing, chosen or imposed, "division of labour" between men and women. We women also want to come out into the light of church history, and we shall do so, not — we hope — out of ambition but for the sake of justice.

Wall decoration for the women's meeting during the WCC's Assembly in Vancouver, 1983.

What we must not do, however, is to pursue the wrong models of power. We must ourselves try patiently and with perseverance to find different and credible ways of exercising "power". We should invite everyone in the church, especially those who hold power at present, to join us in creating this community of footwashers so that together we can find new ways of handling the power entrusted to us. Unless we ourselves are clearly seen to be practising what we preach, the secular world is not likely to take us seriously.

It might help to prevent service in the church from becoming simply the empty phrase it so often is, if we women were to keep in mind a few guidelines and ideas to think about. These might also help anyone who is in a position of authority or responsibility to take this task seriously. Some of the points that occur to me are these:

1. Examine for yourself whether the power you happen to possess is legitimate. Is it a just kind of power?
2. Be ready at any time publicly to give an account of your decisions.
3. "Serving" does not mean having no opinions of one's own; on the contrary it requires a clear commitment to support the weak.
4. Take a critical look at your own use of the outward signs of power. Avoid anything that puts a distance between yourself and your sisters and brothers (e.g. use of titles, inaccessibility, privileges of office, extravagance in terms of dress,

housing, the use of official cars, disproportionate remuneration, insistence on hierarchical procedures, etc.)

5. Try to practise "humility" in your own life in visible ways, so that others can recognize it.
6. Avoid having other people serve you.
7. Try to gather round you a group of people who will be supportive and who are ready to tell you frankly if your manner of serving becomes authoritarian.
8. Involve other people as much as possible in decision-making. Be prepared to share power.
9. Use your power to help other women on their way.
10. Make sure your colleagues have the opportunity to express their criticism openly to you (reciprocity).
11. Work towards putting a time-limit on your mandate. Prepare yourself and others for handing over power.
12. Show that you are self-critical; work and pray.

We need to talk together about these ideas which can no doubt be developed further. This is just the beginning, not the end, of our reflection. I often remind myself and others that we Christians are the only Bible the world ever reads nowadays. If we, of all people, do not believe in the power of love — clearly and for all to see — then who else is going to? Who else will believe in the power of taking first steps, the power of sharing possessions, the power of trust, the power of forgiveness, the power of justice? Big words — too big, perhaps. But they have lost none of their radiance, it seems to me. They still shine out of even our humblest attempts and make visible something of the whole, something of God's kingdom in which we participate with every tentative step we take along the way.

Little kittens

When I saw the four
little black kittens
scramble hungrily
for their mother's tits

and play
with their tiny miaows
their cheeky game
under the settee,

my heart sank.

Where in the future
will
our cat-less
computer-children
draw the desire
to struggle for their mother-earth?

6. Women hold up half the sky

A letter to Elsa

I have a friend in Central America. Elsa is a young woman of 34 who teaches New Testament at a theological seminary. She is married to a man of Indian background who is a liberation theologian; they have two adopted children, one of whom is black. She is a friend with whom I have bathed in hot springs in the mountains, and held long conversations about the global sisterhood. Elsa is very intelligent. She is destined to become one of Latin America's leading theologians, if she is not one already. The dialogue between us is both public and personal. And because the quest for global sisterhood is something we both share I have set out my views on the subject in a letter to Elsa.

Dear Elsa,

I don't know if you have time to read letters like this one. The human condition in Central America where you live is getting harder every day. The flower of your hope, the liberation of Nicaragua, with the delightful pictures of old people carefully tracing the shaky letters patiently and devotedly taught them by the young people, is in danger of being crushed in the stranglehold of "Big Brother" to the North. Everything has become more difficult, even the "radiant hope" that you and José have shown me so vividly and unforgettably. For you, hope is not just a bland word that enables you to drag along, but something from which you draw daily nourishment.

I feel it every time we meet, this love of life and laughter; the enthusiasm with which you work for a better world and for God's kingdom is infectious. Your hope is sustained by the knowledge that in the midst of all your struggles and suffering God is present, eating from the same dish as the poor, that God's sleep is disturbed like yours, and that this gives you a unique opportunity really to meet God face to face.

You say the present time in Latin America is a time of blessing, which sounds crazy to us. But nonetheless it is true, you say, because you no longer have to seek God in intellectual theological structures, nor in the heights of heaven or the depths of the soul or the earth, but have the great good fortune to meet God every day, in the street, at the market, by the roadside, in the fields. Spirituality permeates the whole of your life. This

makes it possible for you to read the Bible with new eyes, the eyes of a Latin American woman, as I know you do. When you sit together at table, priests, nuns, pastors, women, men, sharing your food and discussing your risky pastoral tasks, Jesus is in your midst as he was at Emmaus, because in the sharing of your meagre bread you recognize him. The children of Guatemala fleeing from the murderous bayonets of the militia have no need of an intellectual commentary to help them understand the story of the baby Jesus fleeing into Egypt.

The tears shed by the mothers of Latin America over the coffins of their tortured children are the bitter tears of Mary who, like them, cannot fathom the self-giving life and harrowing death of their sons and daughters. And for the people who gather on a Sunday morning to read out the list of their murdered or missing relatives, answering every name with a loud "presente" (he is here, she is here), the Easter faith is no mere speculation.

In all of this, you tell me, there is a faith and a strength which you can only ascribe to the working of the Holy Spirit. This is what enables people not only to remain human while they are in the stranglehold of power, but to become *more* human, sharing what they have with each other, however little it may be, bread, time, consolation.

But now, Elsa, look at us. New things are happening here too. Much of this has been started by women, in the peace movement, the women's movement, the quest for justice and a new life-style. I know how eagerly you study the books of feminist theologians. I also know that you have great hopes of a "global sisterhood", which was the motto of the women's pre-assembly meeting before the WCC Sixth Assembly in Vancouver. When I spoke to the women who attended it from all over the world, I said that sisterhood is something we have to create and build; it does not simply exist because we happen to be women. I also said it can only come about if it is global, if it includes the human condition of our sisters in Asia, Africa and Latin America, in East and West.

Sisterhood means trying to develop independent relationships among women as something of equal birth and worth alongside brotherhood. I said that we need global sisterhood not against men but for our own sakes.

But what is sisterhood exactly? Is sisterhood something different from brotherhood? Does it have a different tone or range, does it reach higher or go deeper? Is it better, more enduring, more reliable, honest, generous, sensitive than brotherhood? Does it bind us, women, more closely together? Is it in fact true that sisterhood can only be global? Is sisterhood an indispensable stage on the road to full humanity for women and men together? And if so, why? So many questions, so many hopes.

But do you and I really have something to say to each other across the continents, despite social contrasts, despite colonial history, despite the impoverishing aid to your countries? What my contemporaries here are suffering from is depression and helplessness, fear of economic and nuclear disaster, weariness and pain in human relationships, especially between men and women. We women here in Western Europe, after a delay of some 200 years, are in the process of applying the intellectual gains of the Enlightenment and the highly-prized right to human self-determination to ourselves. I expect you know that when a courageous woman like Olympe de Gouges demanded that the slogan "liberty, equality, fraternity" should also apply to women in the Paris of 1793, she was sent to the scaffold by the National Convention. [36]

When in 1776 America made its famous Declaration of Independence and the citizens pompously proclaimed the political right of self-determination, women, Indians, slaves and non-property-owners were not regarded as citizens in the full sense and their demands to be represented, made by people like Abigail Adams,[37] were contemptuously dismissed.

It is only now, in the second half of the twentieth century, that we are beginning to work towards the realization of our full humanity, like so many others to whom it was denied by the supposedly enlightened spirit of the eighteenth century — blacks, native Indians, non-Europeans, the lower classes.

Women's progress towards the realization of their full humanity is now truly underway and the birth pangs are equally difficult for men and women. But there are no alternatives. We do not know yet where it will lead. We are going through deep waters, and the possibilities for error and wrong turnings are many. The goal we are aiming for is not immediately clear, otherwise it would be easy. But it has to grow. Many of us are well aware that this ambitious effort to put the relationship between the sexes on a new basis is not unconnected with preventing humanity from plunging into the abyss.

Even though it would be an over-simplification to deny our passive complicity in the present catastrophic state of our world, we believe nonetheless that new initiatives and alternatives to ensure the continuation of love on our planet earth can be born of women, the half of humanity that has been absent from public life until now. Given the stockpiles of nuclear weapons on our planet, peace can only be achieved today through willingness to compromise — an ability which, as Irmtraud Morgner has put it,[38] has until now been classed as close to cowardice and attributed mainly to women.

You are also aware of the work being done by feminist theologians over here. We are shaking away at the old symbols and systems which have had such a one-sided monopoly in our religious life. We are thinking about an inclusive language for theology and the church. Sometimes, I know, you feel that that is a luxury and I can understand that, though I cannot accept it because language and the images it uses are the reflection of reality — and if women do not feature in the language and symbols used, it means that we are also invisible in the reality they cover.

With great imagination, honesty, longing and anger we have been unmasking the patriarchal structures of our churches, because we believe that the radical message of the gospel cannot be fitted harmoniously into a patriarchal structure.

When in this connection we speak of sisterhood, we are not thinking of it as an alternative to brotherhood — I at any rate do not want to do that — but because we believe women can develop and maintain independent relationships among themselves that are not subject to male approval or disapproval. This happens quite naturally in ecumenical circles, for example the Women's World Day of Prayer. I believe that what women have to do first and foremost is to learn to acknowledge one another as full human beings. To achieve this, we have to work at improving our own low self-esteem and the low value placed on women's activities in our religious and cultural life, and to overcome them in ourselves. Only if we act as though we had some confidence in ourselves, as if we knew our own strength, will we be able to make our contribution to the future of humanity. After all, as Irmtraud Morgner has pointed out, the "present status quo of man is antiquated", and many men suffer as a result of it.

You and I have talked about all these things. I have been delighted to discover how you have been applying your finely honed analytical mind to the situation of women in Latin America. They suffer under a double or even threefold oppression — because they are poor, because they are indigenous, because they are women. More than that, I have been fascinated by all your creative discoveries in the Bible, your reading of the Song of Songs with new eyes, the story of Sarah and Hagar (was it not Hagar, the foreign woman, as much as Abraham to whom God's revelation happened in the loneliness of the desert?), your dialogue with Job.

All of these are things we are able to talk about easily, discovering how much we have in common. But whenever it comes to our search for global sisterhood we invariably touch the sore points where there is friction, misunderstanding, mistrust, where we have never been able to make any headway. This is not just something between you and me. There is a fundamental divide between our countries, our cultures, our histories, which we have not yet been able to bridge despite all our friendship and our common faith in Jesus. There are two sore points in particular which seem to me a long way from being resolved. They divide us like a tear which sometimes, from both sides, we try to mend and sometimes tug apart. Let me try and describe them.

From time to time you ask straight out: is it possible for us to be sisters when you women of the first world withdraw from the social reality in which you live and which drains our life blood, when you sit meditating by candlelight behind closed doors, when you trace the myths of primeval mothers and goddesses in dark valleys, and invoke the life force; when in addition to all you already have you want female spirituality as well. Is it possible for us to be sisters when you enjoy the fruit of our hard labour, when you clothe yourselves in fine silk or casual cotton, without thinking of the stress and strain borne by the Indian seamstresses, while you search for a new spirituality? Is it possible to be sisters, when you are rediscovering the spirituality of your bodies in games and dancing, while the bodies of our women are used to satisfy the desires of your emancipation — weary men in return for payment? Is it possible to be sisters when in your struggle against the missiles you forget that many are already falling victims to the bomb today — in the third world?

As a third-world woman you read the biblical story of Sarah and Hagar as that of the conflict between the childless mistress and the pregnant slave woman. You look upon the social reality between these two women as the operative factor. There you have the one who is privileged and the one without rights. The mistress throws the young woman out because the presence of the child might rob her of her privilege. Sarah is unwilling to share with Hagar. She is unable to recognize her as a sister, to cross social and racial barriers, or to let her ill-fortune touch her conscience. But God sees Hagar. As you say: Hagar does complicate the history of salvation. Is that perhaps our conflict, Elsa? A conflict between the Sarahs of the first world and the Hagars of the third world? Are we guilty of driving you and your children out to die of hunger and thirst in the desert?

You say that we women too are becoming entangled in dead-end Western theology, only reversing the symbols. You say that we are looking for God or rather Goddess — or, if you like, the true meaning of life — in isolation, in abstraction, in individual self, in symbolism, in introspective contemplation, instead of looking in the world around us into which God came, and still comes, God in people and living things, in other words: in the incarnation.

Elsa, you know that in this part of the world we are suffering from a tremendous spiritual barrenness in our lives. Rationalistic religiosity, bloodless dogmatics, and even more a materialistic attitude to life have given rise to the demand for self-realization, for meaning, for contact with the inner self. Women have come to understand that part of the role to which they are subjected is that they are expected always to be available for others — their children, their husband, their boss. Their lives have always been governed by other people, not by themselves. Now they are determined at least to take themselves and their needs seriously, to get to know themselves, and they have a right to do so. I can see you shaking your head thoughtfully and saying: self-determination — of course it is an essential part of every human life.

But it can also become a loveless ideology leading nowhere except back to oneself and that is not enough for life. I fully agree with you; the danger is a real one in our part of the world. But I have no intention of caricaturing the earnest quest of many of our sisters when they say: "How do I find a loving Goddess?" Their courage and determination in breaking open the old symbolic systems are part of the strength we need to help us overcome centuries of rigidity and to find new meaning in the old traditions.

The spiritual sustenance derived from the shared bread, from the shared robe, and from the young people won for life, has not so far found its way into the language of faith in our churches. The language of our Christian tradition over here is not ready to make way for it. It is too well-guarded — if it has not already been dismissed long ago by many who are seeking new ways. That is our dilemma.

If only it were possible for you, Elsa, to help us to develop a spirituality of our own which does not ignore the fact that we are women, yet does not inevitably slip into the cast-off garments of nature religions and mystery cults in order to bring mind, body and soul together on a new level! The questions you are putting to us are very important here. Some of the things women are coming up with on their journeys of discovery today do not quench my thirst for justice and slightly offend my intellect by their anti-rational traits.

The other question that is constantly cropping up in our conversations is a fairly crucial one: what part do men play if what we are aiming for is global sisterhood? Both you and I love and live with a man. And we do not shirk the difficulty of applying the views of the women's movement in many small, sometimes even mean details in our daily lives. It is the price we pay, and pay willingly, in order to find a better alternative to the disintegrated relationship between many partners.

But I know that many women and men are neither willing nor able to do this. I know it from my own experience, too. I do not share the view of some of our sisters in the women's movement, that women are the better human beings. I know myself too well for that. Like the Song of Bread and Roses I believe that the advancement of women is an advance for the whole of humanity. That is why I still insist that women have to make their own analysis of the situation, that we have to join our forces and, with cunning — if necessary — and with determination, deliberately set about putting an end to patriarchal authoritarianism, in order to make way for something that does more justice to all concerned. And we do it for the men's sake as well as our own.

I know you think, and have openly said, that you in Latin America cannot afford to struggle against your men because there is another, greater adversary: oppression, poverty, war. The feminist struggle is, you fear, a North Atlantic device to undermine the common struggle against oppression in general. That is the second split in our discussions. By remarks like that you give me to understand that you still regard the women's struggle in our part of the world as a side issue. A sisterhood which, according to you, is unaware of the quiet but effective oppression practised against others simply by ignoring or disregarding them does not take its own historical experience seriously. What you are saying in effect is that you feel bound to respond to our neglect of the suffering of our sisters in the third world by a refusal to recognize the suffering of women in the first world as suffering. It amounts to saying that there is a hierarchy of suffering: economic oppression, racism, sexism, in that order.

I would stress that we both believe we need global sisterhood in order to get rid of all forms of oppression, not just sexism. Where we have to reach some agreement is on the inherent link between them. What we have in common here is the experience of living in the mud of marginalization which all women share in one form or another. Like you, I regret the lack of sisterhood in women's thinking and attitudes around the world. But how are we to increase it?

My question to you is this: What is the lesson to be drawn from the experience of the French Revolution and the American Independence movement, where human rights meant men's rights, and from the contemporary experiences, for instance, in Zimbabwe's struggle for independence? In Zimbabwe the women fought on equal footing alongside the men in the struggle for liberation. Once it was over, many of them were again relegated to being office assistants to their former comrades at arms. What that says to me is that at every stage along the way out of servitude, we have to attack every form of discrimination which degrades human beings. Because what we are slowly and painfully learning is the principle that no one can be free if all are not free. At the same time we both know how much it would mean if we could increase the global sisterhood in the world, could pool our strength, share our ideas and experiences, encourage one another, point out mistakes and dead-ends, listen seriously to the historical experiences of others and learn from them. Women could be pioneers in inventiveness, sensitivity and courage. Together, we could be a considerable and determined force for the preservation of love on our planet.

And that, Elsa, is why there must be room for this dialogue in your daily life — as in mine. That is why we must share these thoughts with all our sisters involved in the same quest; that little word "global" is our responsibility. We cannot solve conflicts or avoid them by escaping to another planet, either as nations or as individual women and men, because this is the only world we have. There is therefore no alternative to that little word "global"!

I know we cannot appropriate the word "sisterhood" for our Christian tradition alone, especially when you think how little the voice of women is heard in our churches. But no one should use it without being aware of the biblical dimension of "shalom", the mental-spiritual-physical wellbeing of the whole community, which includes the men and the children. Maybe another distinctive quality in sisterhood, as compared to brotherhood, could be that it is not exclusive in the way it is practised. Sisterhood would then be the friendship and compassionate love for all living things shown by women collectively and in their relationships with one another, and it would serve to improve the quality of life of all of us — without sidestepping the issue of justice. As the quality characteristic of one half of humanity it would be an indispensable part of the vision of a new heaven and a new earth.

If sisterhood is understood in this sense, then the adjective "global" really becomes unnecessary, because no one would work at one part without keeping the whole in mind. I would love to be able to promise you that our new spirituality and sisterhood have you and your friends, men and women, very much at heart; in other words, it is ecumenical in the deepest sense. We are doing a lot of thinking about how it all belongs together.

Dear Elsa, at the risk of sounding sentimental, I want to end my letter with this thought: Let us keep sewing away at the tear in the mantle of sisterhood so that we may turn it into something whole, something more honest, more all-embracing, more lasting in which we can wrap the cold, hungry, trembling earth and bring new life to the worried and confused people on it. Can we agree on that? Then let us try!

7. Liberation stories...

During my ecumenical wandering-years, women have shared many stories with me, and many images and circumstances of women's lives are in my mind's eye. I have retained them in my heart and in my head. Many of them, of course, I have been able to keep alive through the unerring eye of my camera. Now that all these pictures are as it were spread out before me, they combine to explain our women's story, brimful of fear, distortion, crying needs, brutality and failure. Yet at the same time there are the stories and pictures of liberation, healing, acceptance, walking-tall, courage, determination, joy at being alive, the will to live, sisterhood. Something has happened there, giving rise to a movement, a movement in the direction of becoming free.

Because I read the Christian tradition with my feminine eyes nowadays, I recognize in our own women's story (as many women have done before me) the biblical story of the healing of the crippled woman. And so I put all the pieces of my discovery of the women's world together until those many stories, alongside the biblical story, become one complete story, or picture, in which all of us feature somewhere, as those who are crippled, healing, made whole, giving thanks.

"One Sabbath Jesus was teaching in a synagogue and there was a woman there possessed by a spirit that had crippled her for eighteen years. She was bent double and quite unable to stand up straight" (Luke 13:10-13).

For centuries, we women have been possessed by a spirit that used to cripple us. Throughout history it fed itself on the privilege of male interpretation and culture. It thrived on life's harsh constraints humiliatingly inflicted especially on women. We ourselves also fed it with our internalized weakness and lack of self-worth, with the talents we decided not to make available, with the sacrifices made (though not of our own free will), with the magic cloak that makes our real self invisible. We did not count, we just faded into the dark of history, in childbirth, kitchens and sitting rooms. The evil spirit of female weakness caused us to be bowed down and bent double.

And so I see before my eyes:

— The women in Thailand; knee-deep in water, they are planting rice, bent double all their life to produce a little food, so that they may survive, they and the children, so that they need not flee to the big city.

— The mother in Soweto, bent double with grief over her child, shot down. She had brought it into the world hoping for better times.

— The women in industry at the assembly lines of the multi-nationals, their backs bent over the small components they have to assemble, and which give no meaning to their lives as women.

— The women behind the veils of a piously prescribed chastity, their eyes with shame averted in the face of curiosity. That is how it has always been and always will be, say the Mullahs.

— And those without any veils at all, on naked display in Manila, vulnerable and exposed before lustful stares — and not just stares. Money will buy anything.

— The mother with four children, looking for shelter in a sewer, as long as it does not rain. A few rags protect her, that is all; until the next rain.

— The woman refugee, with bag and baggage; the husband happens to be on the wrong side in the war. Her meagre possessions — a cooking pot, a blanket — dwindling as she flees, and the unknown country will bring yet more humiliations.

— The woman giving birth on the pavement in an Indian city; worn out, her puny baby in a plastic bag in the midst of dust and stench. Who is going to bother about them?

— The water-carriers; from miles away they are hauling the precious liquid in jars on both shoulders — to do the laundry for strangers. Maybe there will be some left for their own washing.

— The desperate one, her hands covering her face. Her husband has gone, away to the city, leaving her without saying good-bye, without any promises. The burden of field work, looking after the animals, the children, now lies on her shoulders alone. He ran away out of desperation, leaving her alone with no way out.

— The seamstresses, row upon row of them; sewing luxurious dresses for a pittance. Hardly a word is spoken, though there would be so much to say; the whirring of the sewing machines is the only sound to be heard; so much sweat for the beauty of other women in Europe and America adorning themselves without giving it a second thought. Where are they, the sisters?

— The bearers of heavy baskets full of sand and stones; they are staggering under them day in and day out, for a few measly rupees, with the supervisor behind them. To satisfy his lust, he will not hesitate to pick one out — any quiet corner will do.

— The black maid in the white lady's house in Capetown, where she washes and cleans, makes children who are strangers laugh, bowed down with yearning for love and human closeness. Her own children back in the homeland are starving.

— The old woman, rummaging through stinking rubbish, looking for anything of value, anything edible, perhaps, that she might pull out of the muck. What is left of human worth? How can one retain one's self-respect — after that?

— The woman living in fear of her husband's beatings. He is unemployed and spends his last cent on drink at his local. When he comes home, he shouts, and beats her, and forces his daughter into bed with him. And she has to stand there and watch, biting her fingers till they bleed, sobbing: O my God!

— Those who are hiding; horror just outside the door, they are listening for the soldier's footsteps, for the plunging of bayonets into the front door, for steps and shouts. Hiding will be no good; defenceless they will be slashed open.

— The forgotten one, Camille Claudel, lover and source of inspiration of the great master Rodin, the giant. Her sculptures are beautiful, majestic, playful, as good as his. Together they created many things over the years. He remained famous, she died in misery, her work long ignored, until recently.

That is how I see her in my mind's eye — with her fear of the future, of being alone, of being deserted, with the fear that drains the marrow from her bones, turning her into a mere shadow of herself. No God, no Goddess looks upon her. Woman, who are you, so bent double and unable to stand up straight?

"When Jesus saw her he called her and said: 'You are rid of your trouble.' Then he laid his hands on her."

Something flows across, a wave of love and power, recognition and becoming whole, healing for body and soul. Someone has seen her, at long last. Her eyes encounter a human face. She stands up straight, a daughter of God, put at the same level with her whole-maker, with the others!

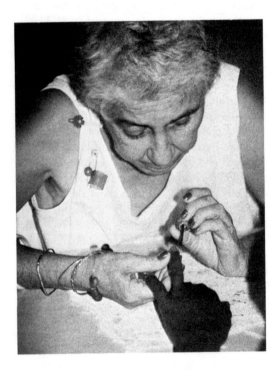

Where God is at work through the hand of the sister, the brother, where we help each other, lovingly touch each other, desolateness fades away and we raise each other up.

Those scenes, too, I see before my eyes:

— In front of me there is a picture of Chinese women workers, putting arms around each other during the afternoon break. It gives strength for the next round of work and living.

— Unforgettable is for me the scene in a beauty salon of the psychiatric clinic in Havana: a disturbed patient with tousled head makes another one beautiful — painting her fingernails red, giving her a magnificent hair-do, so that she can carry herself with beauty into the darkness of insanity.

— Or the woman doctor in the bush, injection needle against the child's skin, fighting against fever, blindness; life-giving touch.

— Or the women's refuge in a West German city, where the telephones keep ringing and cries for help meet with a response: a bed, protection, safe accommodation and counselling for the next steps.

— A woman and a man — for a little while the outside world is forgotten, touching, only you and I, before life invades and separates again.

— Together the African women pound the yam roots to pulp, in a rhythmic one-after-another, full of community, in a common bond against hunger.

"Then at once she straightened up and began to praise God."

She stands up straight and needs someone whom she can thank. We women are today standing up straight and are beginning to live, to think, to act. The Spirit that used to cripple us is withdrawing, has left us. The pictures I see before me also include these:

— The rebellious nuns of America, who will no longer allow themselves to be pushed around by regulations decreed from "the very top", because they have changed from being minors into thinking human beings who cannot go back again. They are acting on their own responsibility, in the light of their own faith.

— The peace women in England, taking root in the face of missile bases, their feminine determination making those in command unsure of themselves. They are standing upright.

— Women who break bread and share the cup with each other, though often still in secret. Since Jesus raised us up, who can possibly stop us? What is holiest of all, given into women's hands.

— The Babushka sneaking into church, kneeling before the priest and secretly bringing her grandchild for baptism. The laughter of her gold teeth lighting up her pious face, she is the truly indestructible woman, who has been walking tall and upright for decades. One day the priests will at last bow down in homage to her and her faithfulness. She has time and can wait.

— The women of Kenya, planting trees against the desert and against hunger, united with each other as "women of the world for development and the environment". They just make simple beginnings — planting, tending future forests, the life of generations yet to come. However much their work makes them bend down, they are walking tall.

— The Theas who will no longer accept what male language, male symbols, a purely male religion would want to dictate to them. They are discovering the secret roots of female piety and bring to light a new language of the faith in a frightened church.

— Women working at conveyor belts are organizing themselves, walking out of the places that used to cripple them, speaking of their self-worth, their wages.

— Women against the bank, words against gold. Has anyone ever seen such a thing? How they are carrying placards, the women for South Africa, calling for a boycott, and depositing the golden calf outside the bank, where it belongs. What are the insults of one bank against the decisions of a bank? (free after Brecht)

— Mothers in the Pacific: after nuclear tests they have given birth to jelly-fish babies, a formless bag, breathing. Now they are shouting it from the rooftops: you spoilers of our seas, our fish, our beaches, our children. Test your bombs in Paris, store them in Washington, bury your nuclear waste in Tokyo, if it is so safe!

— The African mother, her baby on her arm, addressing 3000 church people from all over the world, speaks to the glory of God of giving birth, of blood and sweat, of life as a gift entrusted to us by God. She will send her daughter into the future walking tall.

— The old Indian woman, surrounded by women who had come from far to hear her share the age-old wisdom of her people, who are historically on the side of the losers. She addresses those listening to her as daughters and granddaughters, and her voice trembles, but she walks upright and praises Mother Earth.

— My own mother, an old woman, seventy-six years young, who once a week gets together with two of her daughters — also grey already — to teach them to play the guitar, in order that the human race will not forget how to sing...

The history of all these women will have to be written afresh, by all of them together, arising out of their experience. It must become part of the history of our human race, in which future generations will be able to recognize the courage and faith of their fore-mothers and -fathers, and be guided by them so that they may go on living and working. Today we are looking for the point of contact in the story of the women. We will never again allow the biblical stories and all other liberation stories to be taken away from us.

Many women and men draw inspiration and strength from a song from the early days of the women's movement. The first to raise the demand for "Bread and Roses" were women workers, when they began to resist the imposition of harsh working conditions and through this simple formulation held on to a great goal for the human family. Again and again it is the simple things that are the goals for which to work, to struggle, to love, to pray, to argue and to sing. And where women become free, where they are being liberated from meaningless and crippling slavery, the whole of humanity will become more free.

Bread and Roses

As we come marching, marching
in the beauty of the day,
a million darkened kitchens,
a thousand mill lofts grey,
are touched with all the radiance
that a sudden sun discloses.
For the people hear us singing,
"Bread and Roses, Bread and Roses".

As we come marching, marching,
we battle, too, for men,
for they are women's children
and we mother them again,
our lives shall not be wasted
from birth until life closes,
hearts starve as well as bodies:
give us bread but give us roses.

As we come marching, marching,
unnumbered women dead
go crying through our singing
their ancient songs of bread.
Small art and love and beauty
their drudging spirits knew.
Yet, it is bread we fight for,
but we fight for roses, too.

As we come marching, marching,
we bring the Greater Days,
the rising of the women means
the rising of the race.
No more the drudge and idler,
ten who toil where one reposes,
Bread and Roses, Bread and Roses. [39]

8. The difficulty and ease of having images of God

Confusion of tongues

What word of human speech is so misused, so defiled, so desecrated as this (the word *God*)! All the innocent blood that has been shed for it has robbed it of its radiance. All the injustice that it has been used to cover has effaced its features...

Yes, it is the most heavy-laden of all human words. None has become so soiled, so mutilated. Just for this reason I may not abandon it. Generations of men have laid the burden of their anxious lives upon this word and weighed it to the ground; it lies in the dust and bears their whole burden... But when all madness and delusion fall to dust, when they stand over against Him in the loneliest darkness and no longer say "He, He" but rather sigh "Thou", shout "Thou", all of them the one word, and when they then add "God", is it not the real God whom they all implore, the One Living God, the God of the children of Man?... We cannot cleanse the word "God" and we cannot make it whole; but, defiled and mutilated as it is, we can raise it from the ground and set it over an hour of great care. [40]

With a commitment like this Martin Buber set himself against an age which has entered into the "eclipse of God". Everything had been thought through. The "wisdom of the wise" had come to an end (1 Cor. 1:19). They had struggled through all possible hypotheses about God: Aristotle, Augustine, Plato, Thomas Aquinas, Spinoza, Kant, Hegel, Heidegger, and whoever else down the centuries.

They had relegated God to the realms above and below, to the within and the beyond, as almighty, supreme, the immovable mover, the hidden one, as man, as the wholly other, as ultimate reason, as *deus ex machina* (the God who suddenly turns up when you need him), until finally they had gone through the whole range of possibilities, and the most radical in their ranks (Nietzsche) cried out: "God is dead... and we have killed him." It is simply impossible to "take him apart", let alone "put him together". It is too much a matter of "sour grapes" to us; we do not need him any longer.

The conceivable God could no longer be conceived. And anything you cannot describe intellectually, or comprehend or define, cannot possibly exist, says the thinker. There he sits: cast in bronze by Rodin, unable to think any further. The God they wanted to annex within their concepts had emigrated away from the names they had invented and the thoughts with which they had experimented, away from their metaphysics. (Was there ever a time when God really existed in that realm?)

I, too, have rushed through the centuries, eagerly treading the paths of the great thinkers, discovering their discoveries for myself, suffering the defeats they suffered, and putting the lid on the coffin of the God whom they thought they could catch in the net of our human concepts and ideas. With the presaging Hölderlin, I too have cried out in the cold of the soul's winter: "Woe unto me! Where do I, when it is winter, find the flowers, where the sunshine and the shadows cast on the earth?"[41] The only thing I was able to cling to, during my human and spiritual experience of the eclipse of God, was the questioning hunger in the eyes of a black child, condemning all this darkness as a lie — it was in those very eyes that God clearly came across to me.

This is how I want to raise, preserve that desecrated, sullied, torn-up word "God". I want to help lift it up in my own way not just to set it over an hour of great care. No, I also want to set it over hours of great happiness and high emotion.

I want to set it over the hours of extreme intensity, and of slow break-through; the hours of self-discovery and devotion, the hours of truth, the hours of the incarnation of human beings — their becoming truly human.

Of course there is little one can do against the inflation of the word "God" caused by the market pedlars of religion. If only I can avoid being lumped together with them, I sometimes think, refusing stubbornly to adopt the language they prattle in — with good intentions, no doubt, but with such deadly emptiness.

"Do you really believe in the kind of God with whom you can scare little children?" Emma Biermann, the communist, once asked me straight. "No, I do not believe in such a God," I quickly replied. "That's all right then."

It is probably pointless to trace the various worn-out images of God through the centuries, which have been peeled off like onion skins by the discoveries of astronomy, geography, philosophy, physics, medicine, economics, politics. In order for the world to function, we no longer need God as a moral, political, scientific, philosophical or religious working hypothesis. That was the last thing Dietrich Bonhoeffer said to the world he left — the man of faith in prison, faced with death.[42]

Nevertheless, all these images of God are there at all time. Many of them have never been divulged to the faithful by the church. One of the effects of the disparity among contemporaries, who are living off the accumulated store of many and varied centuries, is that we are unable to share with each other what we mean, without clearly talking things out. So this is exactly what we should do, because too many people think of God as the one who, hidden in the clouds, observes us down below and intervenes in matters we have long been capable of managing on our own.

The image of God that went out with the Ptolemaic concept of the world still permeates and carries the atheism of our day with disastrous consequences. To show how complicatedly simple this is, I want to tell you about a brief encounter I once had.

On a flight from the Caribbean to Europe I sit next to a well-tanned Russian. His particular devotion to work had been rewarded with a holiday in Cuba. He is in a good mood and wants to start a conversation with me straightaway. But what language shall we use? I know no Russian, and he only has ten words of German. Impossible to communicate? But he will not give up, and so the following conversation takes place:

He asks: "Tourista?"
I say: "No, conference."
"Aha," he says. Then he draws a fish on a newspaper that is lying in front of us. He is asking about the theme of the conference.

I draw a church on the paper.
He is wide-eyed with amazement.
He used what is obviously the Russian
word for church with a big question mark. "How church?"
He points to me and asks: "Work?"

I draw myself in a preaching gown.
He shakes his head incredulously.
He cannot get that into his head,
which is used to Orthodox priests only.

And then he says: "Nix God — God no!"
I say: "God — yes!"
He explains, as best he can, that the sputnik has flown to heaven, but that there was no God up there.
He then proceeds to make the following little drawing:

I say: "God is not in the clouds, he is in your own heart for instance." I draw a heart on the paper and point to his own heart.

He does not believe me and laughs, and clutches his chest. "God no — see nothing!"

I should like to tell him that there are many things one cannot see, but which we experience, like love for instance. "Love," he says, "but my wife...." he shows me that he can touch her.
I draw a globe and say: "God is everywhere."

How does one continue such a dialogue? He writes number 1979 on the paper. Then he points to the church. Then he writes down 1990 and crosses out the church. I see: so the church will disappear. I draw another church next to the number 1990. He laughs. "God — no!" he says.

Then he tells me about a book he once read in which it said that the stories in the Bible are fairy-tales. So he had laughed.

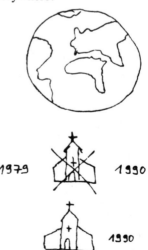

He demonstrates how he used to laugh. But his grandmother would tell him that he must not laugh.

His grandmother still believed in that Bible stuff. Suddenly he thinks of the word "fool". He says that I am a fool when I say "God — yes!" He asks me whether we make the sign of the cross with two or three fingers. By crossing out the hand I tell him that we do not use that symbolic gesture at all. That does not contribute much to mutual understanding.

He points to my red-painted toe-nails and says: "God — no!" I tell him that my toe-nails do not disturb God. Meanwhile he has ordered a bottle of champagne. We are drinking the champagne and he thinks that that would not please God either.

A young Russian student who speaks French comes over to us and explains to his compatriot that he had met many Marxists in France who are also Christians. The man next to me thinks it is all very funny and he shakes his head incredulously. Once more he attempts to convince me. He explains that the plane can take off and land without God. "God is asleep," he says.

He tells me that during the war he fought against the Germans. I say that my father, too, had fought in Russia, and that many German men had died there. "Why did they come to Russia? They should have stayed in Germany," he says.

Then we change the subject and talk about other things. Sometimes he looks at me half amused, half doubtful. From time to time he again says: "God — no!" When we get to Frankfurt we say good-bye, warmly: "German woman — friendship."

That was the first Russian I ever met personally. What an interesting dialogue we had about the existence of God! What a strange image of God he had! Hence all this atheism? He only enquired about a *thing*, whereas I spoke of an *experience*. A real Babel! If only we could overcome this misunderstanding — I think to myself with excitement — then we would not have to destroy the world; at least there would not be so many people engaged in these deadly exploits, who would follow the ideological pied piper. It became very clear to me in that conversation that "God" is more than the metaphysical capital of human knowledge, accumulated over the centuries and deposited in a bank of faith. When you want to withdraw it, it turns

out to be no more than threshed straw. All ontological pronouncements are a waste of energy. Maybe there was a time
when they were necessary, but it is no longer so. Nevertheless
there are these people who obstinately maintain — and I am one
of them — that they have come face to face with God.
Throughout the centuries there have been people who have
borne witness to the untiring longing to relate to someone,
something, outside themselves, something that is really true,
something that is truly clear, important, eternal.

After going through the eclipse of God we have — it is true —
stopped asking: "What is God like?" But we have not stopped
asking: "Where do we meet God?" What does God mean for our
life? Measured against centuries of spiritual development which
has slowly reached the point of no longer asking questions about
the typical characteristics of God, or about proof of God's existence, it does appear to be a little old-fashioned when women these
days are demanding the recognition of the femaleness of God. As
an enquiry into a qualitative being it has no validity. But there is of
course another level, namely that of the ways in which we experience God. After the eclipse of God, the question "Where do we
meet God?" opens a new door for us Western people, through
which maybe the light of God can again come streaming in.

Many people are looking for this crack of the door, among
them many women with their discoveries about the female half
of God.

You shall not make an image for yourself

> For God was passing by: a great and strong wind came rending
> mountains and shattering rocks before him, but God was not in the
> wind; and after the wind there was an earthquake, but God was not
> in the earthquake; and after the earthquake fire, but God was not in
> the fire; and after the fire a low murmuring sound. When Elijah
> heard it, he muffled his face in his cloak and went and stood at the
> entrance of the cave. Then there came a voice... (1 Kings 19:11-
> 13).

For Elijah at this point in his life, God was in the low
murmuring sound. He was prepared to hear God in that. To
Moses, God spoke in a burning bush, to Jacob in the dream of a
ladder to heaven; to Hagar in the crying of her child dying of
thirst; to Balaam through an ass; to Job in a thunderstorm; to

Jeremiah God spoke through almond blossom; to Paul through a light from heaven; to Mary through an angel. They were all prepared to let God into their life.

Is there any reason to suppose that God is not still using the variety of nature to address us? Through our dreams, whose coded messages people are anxious to decipher nowadays in order to get in touch with, and to sort out, the dark and hidden sides of their existence. Through the world of nature, its beauty, its power or violation, through wind and clouds, in the whisper of the waves, in the silence, in pictures and music — or should God have restricted him/herself to one hour's worth of male pronouncements on a Sunday morning?

The clearest way in which God still speaks to us is through human beings, through his/her people sent to meet us on our way today. After all, God went out of the way to experience our human lot from within, so as to share him/herself with us and in order that there might be no ambiguity. For it is — you will agree — not easy to distinguish when God is speaking, or when it is our own desires, our masochism, or persons laying down the law, acting like wolves in sheep's clothing.

The God of the Bible journeys with his/her creatures, through their history and their affairs. This is why God does not always remain the same, any more than they do. And yet God remains true to him/herself. Is the jealous God of the creation story who does not wish people to become like him/herself, this God of the nomadic shepherds, the same as the One who enters into a covenant relationship with the runaway slaves? A covenant binding also him/herself? Is it the same God who inspires the politically experienced prophet Isaiah to speak about the suffering servant? And is this God the same as the One who as a carpenter's son cries aloud in his god-forsakenness on the cross?

The only thing that God, Yahweh, reveals of him/herself to the people of the Old Testament who are urgently reaching out for security, is that description which even today we are still trying to decipher. Martin Buber, whom in this case I would credit with a superior knowledge of Hebrew, translates this statement to Moses as: "I shall be there as the one who will be there". I do not wish to be pedantic here, but a lot depends on this. A lot of ontological discussions have been triggered off by this, not least when it was translated as "I am who I am", thus giving the existence of God a merely philosophical foundation. The question as to the *presence* of God is of an entirely different order from that of the *existence* of God. The Hebrew word "Yahweh" after all describes an open, not yet completed but still ongoing activity; it is not something that is static, dormant or abstract.

No neat definition of God's nature, but rather: I shall be there for you. I shall remain the one whom you can experience, the one who acts, the one who comes to meet you.[43] This is the very foundation of our trust in God. That is all that is being said; nothing about how, when or where. It is not much, but how much it is! We cannot tie God down with the fetters of definition, or impose limitations. God does not turn into a manageable substance. No clay is modelled into an idol. No name is divulged by which to swear or through which to rule. The only thing we are assured of is this unfailing possibility of experiencing God, that is all. All the rest remains wide open. The second commandment, "You shall not make a carved image for yourself", is a barrier against any attempts by dogmatists, priests and philosophers to grab God for themselves or to make God serve their own purposes.

Admittedly, people have always expressed their experience of God in the images of human language. What else did they have at their disposal to express what cannot be put into words? And because in a patriarchal society only men have the right to speak, it is not surprising that male words crept into our world of images.

This contrasts sharply with the discovery of a little friend of mine who once wanted to compliment his mother on the lovely sandwiches she had prepared for him when he was hungry. The more sandwiches she made, the higher rose his praise: "You are the most wonderful mummy... in Germany... in Europe... in the whole world." When he appeared to run out of superlatives, he paused and thought for a while and asked: "*Who* says that God is a man?" In order to praise the generosity of his mother, he wants to fall back on God. In order to imagine the generosity of God, he uses his experience with his mother. But what he says about his experience comes up against an ontological definition of God.

Any image we use has a limiting effect. That is how we as women experience it, or rather, that is how we can describe it: the exclusively male images of God are keeping us away from many possible experiences of God, and lock God away in an ontological male shrine from which the men derive their identity and supremacy.

No one is allowed to touch that, apparently. But God is there, wherever God wills. From the ways in which people, including Jesus, described their experience of God — God as a father — they went on to forge statements about who God actually was — he was male. It was precisely against this kind of thing that Yahweh on Horeb protected him/herself. Who would want to prescribe how God should manifest him/herself — whether in a revelation to women in childbirth, in the way women experience the embrace of love, in the magnitude of a discovery, in the beauty of sisterhood, in their courage to walk upright?

Who would want to prevent God from speaking to us through different, new, old symbols? The Spirit blows where he/she/it wills. Where life is being made possible, God cannot be far away. The spirit of Jesus was broader than the spirit of those who administer the legacy he left behind. The way one experiences the female side of God, who like a woman in the parable lights a lamp to look for us, lost coins, God who wipes away our tears, takes us under her wings, prepares a table before us and fills our cup to the brim — all these images of the femininity of God are contained in the Bible, but they never entered into the language of tradition, least of all into the definitive statements of the theologians and philosophers; very few of them made it into the experiential knowledge of our prayers.

"But how about Jesus, of whom we say that he is God in human form: was he not male?" asks the final triumphalist question. Yes, he was a man, but most certainly not the type who would use arguments like that. Do we call Jesus "Child of God" because he was a man or — as it says in the letter to the Philippians — because he became a human being (2:5-8: hymn to Christ)? All further arguments hinge on that. If it is intrinsically necessary to tie God down to his maleness in order to save the world, then it is no more than logical that women should turn the whole thing round and say: a male redeemer cannot redeem women. This is how the absolutizing of one thing leads to the absolutizing of another. Such a thought-pattern reached and still reaches its culmination in women being barred from the priesthood. It was not only justified on the basis of tradition ("things have always been thus") but also by saying that there should be a physical likeness between the priest and Christ — a thought that encourages obscene ideas, and makes clear at the same time how thin the ice is on which the — admittedly powerful — champions of such traditions are skating. "Christianity is being split by women in the pulpit," it was said by a gathering of ordained men.[44] But in reality it is the men in the pulpit who for 2000 years have been splitting the church; who could deny that?

I want to leave it to those who claim that Jesus is the messiah by virtue of his maleness to present their dubious theological arguments, not evading Paul's refutation that in Christ there is neither male nor female. The burden of proof for such stupid claims lies firmly on the shoulders of those who have something to lose.

Knowing God means imitating God

There is a great new search for images of God and Goddess. "What kind of an image are you looking for?" is the question put by the sellers of devotional objects in that supermarket where the meaning of life is on offer, and where shamelessly and with an eye for business they are taking advantage of people's deepest longings.

For goodness sake, have done with this commercialization! One doesn't know what is genuine and what is *kitsch* any more. We are being overwhelmed by much that is beautifully felt, profoundly thought out, aesthetically fashioned, genuinely experienced; but where in all these things is God really *present*, as promised? The church, too, has to compete nowadays, having lost the monopoly of God-language a long time ago. For many people the church has become wooden, wet, empty and depressing.

"How an angel would trample it down beyond trace, their market of comfort, with the church alongside, bought ready for use: as clean and disenchanted and shut as the post on a Sunday!" says Rilke in his *Duino Elegies*.[45] But people are not that easily fobbed off. They want living images of God, encounters with God, which they will be able to distinguish from idols and golden calves.

In this context, one thing is particularly important for our search: in the transition between the Old Testament and the New, the Bible breaks the commandment about images. For despite all absence of images, on one occasion God changed into an image, a likeness. We have an original image of God before us in the poverty of the man Jesus, who was so rich that he could give everything away, including being Lord and being equal with God.[46] For that he committed his life — and lost it — and regained it. So now we have an image of God which is at the same time the image of the true human being, as he/she was intended to be; this God who lost himself completely in world history and thus remained faithful to what Yahweh had promised long ago: "I shall be there, I shall be there for others, be there for you, be with you always, to the end of time, not run away, not vanish when the need is greatest." In the mirror of this human life we are better able to see the reflection of God him/herself: not an olympic God, no Prometheus, no elusive Pan, but a simple, humble God, capable of suffering, with a clear message about the good, true, eternal life.

In visiting the market of God and Goddess images of our own and all previous centuries, we also discover the marks that are associated with the spirit of Jesus and many seekers after God: woman and man made in God's likeness, justice, forgiveness, love: love of oneself, one's neighbour, one's enemy; shalom, peace, purity of heart, readiness for risk and sacrifice, love of creation, community, hope, sharing.

All these great words are to be found even in the small change of everyday life. One mark that should emphatically not be missing is that of God's openness, God who can again and again be found in many-varied manifestations in the present, and not just in the past. Thus equipped, going round the market of the meaning of life does not become any easier, but it is more purposeful. Of course, an ultimate guarantee of really meeting God is nowhere to be had; even in the reciting of the ancient formulas there is no guarantee. After all, Jesus himself says unmistakably: "Not everyone who calls me Lord, Lord, will enter the kingdom of heaven" (Matt. 7:21). But one thing we do know, and that is that a truly genuine encounter cannot be pretended.

As far as I am concerned, I have always found that in the quest for God people tried to prove, lay down or teach too much, and I will have no part in it. I prefer sticking to the Jewish tradition which says: to know God means to imitate God's deeds. But I have been struck by two things that seem to be typical of all biblical encounters with God. There might well be many more.

First of all: the people who have come face to face with God know better who they are themselves.

Secondly: they are given a message to pass on.

On the first point, Schalom Ben Chorin[47] has this to say when commenting on the text: "So God created human beings in his/her own image; in the image of God created them male and female" (Gen. 1:27). If you take this really seriously, then God must be an androgynous being (hermaphrodite), combining within itself male and female in equal proportions. However, the Jews are very strict in refusing to think of God in human images (anthropomorphic). I share this viewpoint where ontological statements are concerned, but I do not share it where such images are an expression of experiences. People who have had an encounter with God have come to know themselves better, as in a mirror (1 Cor. 13:12).

There are many different ways in which we can find out who we are by looking into the God-mirror. Hagar, Abraham's slave girl, bears her witness in the desert: "Have I indeed seen God and still live after that vision?" (Gen. 16:13). Now she knows who she is, a slave girl whom God has chosen, for God has looked upon her and given her a place in the history of salvation. She knows what God wants, for God has made it known to her. The desert became the place of discovery.

And I want rather to insist on this, that there are many different ways of discovering our divine likeness. We women especially have a great deal of catching up to do. You see, one of the female sins we are guilty of is that we do not really believe that we are God's image; we are only a kind of "afterthought" on the part of the creator. Today though, at the end of the twentieth century, we have reached the point where we are encountering and discovering this diversity, God and ourselves, in this mirror, where we are re-discovering and imitating the varied range of God's speech and gestures, where we want to be God's mirrored image.

On the inside of my front door I had for a long time a poster of the small gold woman's statue of Selket, which they had found in a pharaoh's tomb. Every morning, Selket used to greet me on my way out to work with this saying: "I have seen that which was of yesterday, I know that which will be of tomorrow." And I would anwer her:

> With unwavering open arms
> you, proud beauty of the Nile,
> are still emerging from the caverns.
> Your eyes full of boldness,
> your golden body unashamed.
> You know all about tombs.
> And that is why you are able
> to give me strength
> as I move out into the future.

With her obvious resoluteness she has given me a lot of strength for the daily struggles for the dignity of women. She refused, however, to compete with the other symbols in my home or in myself. She did not need to, nor would I have let her.

Often in the silence there arise images which God entrusted to us from of old, many of them described in the Bible. For instance the image that we are God's temple.[48] Amazingly, God sends a human being who with loving hands, looks, words, establishes my divine likeness, and raises my body — by history and by myself so hurt and despised — to be God's temple, in which God can be at home. In the light of such images, the gates to a new self-confidence are being opened wide. We do what Paul tells us: to honour God with eyes, ears, hands, feet, head, kidneys, womb, with the whole of the body (1 Cor. 6:20). I can then also enter into myself and experience the glory or the dreadfulness of God within me, the silence of the soul, the flaring up of the blood, laughter, the taking of risks, the being-in-touch with the hidden, the fear of being forsaken, the fury.

We are God's temple, we women, a women's temple, a sacred place, beautiful and pure, where treasures lie dormant and life is stored up, and where there are sacrifices, too. Mirroring myself in the female side of God I now know better who I am as a created being, a woman, a human being. My opportunities are opened wide with all my pores. Jesus has devoted himself to the restoration of this human temple, especially that of the women. He has taken away their hurts, raised them up, pronounced them clean. He has replaced the stone temple with God's temple, with human beings, and has let the people know that God wants to come and live within them. Our heart will be God's cradle, our body God's workshop.

No one has put it more beautifully than Gioconda Belli, the poet-fighter from Nicaragua. Her woman's confession of faith can pluck us out of all faintheartedness!

And God made me a woman
with long hair,
eyes,
nose and mouth of a woman.
With rounded hills
and folds
and soft depths
he hollowed out my inner self
and turned me into a human workshop.
Intricately interweaving my nerves,
he carefully balanced
my hormones.
Mixed my blood
and poured it into me
so that it might refresh
my body everywhere.
And so the thoughts arose,
the dreams,
the instincts.
All that God gently created
with the rhythm of his breath,
with penetrating love,
the thousand and one things,
that daily make me into a woman,
this is why with pride each morning I awake
and bless the sex to which I belong. [49]

But there is also that other thing, closely related to what has just been said: all encounter with God contains a message within it, a commission, however deeply hidden.

"Go... and say... and do..."

Many people think that they have met God, but they come back without a task. Many people simply want to stay in God's presence. I believe that God does not enter into an encounter simply for his/her own sake. Being with God only means drawing strength for being told what God wants us to do. God communicates, shares him/herself with us, but also ropes us in, makes use of us, makes us God's co-workers (1 Cor. 3:9).

God communicating with us always means God enabling, empowering those whom he/she meets. Hagar saves her child, Moses liberates his people, Mary goes to Elizabeth, Jesus goes to Jerusalem. All these are roads towards a hard but beautiful freedom. Such challenges accompany encounters with God. After such encounters nothing remains as it is. Standing on the threshold of my eclipse of God it seemed to me as if I had received such a communication. The hunger in the eyes of a black child told me, without saying a word: "Go and tell your people, your church, your family, your nation, yourself: 'racism is a sin, hunger is a sin, sexism is a sin'." A bit of biblical pathos like this is good for our frigid and collected souls. It is a help to us to find the biblical images in our life again. The same communication was also shared with me in other encounters. How is it that I know it was the voice of God? Because God came to satisfy the hungry, to let the broken victims go free, to proclaim recovery of sight to the blind (Luke 4).

The world becomes a *thou*; we enter into an *I-thou* relationship which contains God, says Martin Buber. A communication from God can arise out of everything and anything. God goes all out to reach people on their way. And there are still enough obstinate asses around, who are able to make clear to the Balaams of this world what God has to say to them (Num. 22:1-35).

The spirit which used to want to capture God through intellectual processes is called to humility. Of course, we should not abandon the discipline of thinking — God forbid! — but we should stop pretending that that has a claim to exclusive representation, so to speak. After all, God also communicates with us through the mouth of young children and babies and women and asses. Similarly, in the speech of the God-illiterates who do not even know this word or want to know it any longer, but whose images and ways of life speak of God:[50] feminine, masculine, childlike, natural, down-to-earth. There are many images and deeds which have this in common that they point to the realm of God.

And so, after the eclipse of God of the philosophers and theologians we have reached a clearing again, in order that one may know: this is something new.

Faith-mother,
you, Russian,
I have your image before me.
You embody resistance.
Your wrinkles full of sadness.
Has anyone ever seen
a more unbending humility?
It is God
who wove infinity
into your gaze.

In the dirt of human history
you have not lost your devout heart.
With torn hands you dragged it
through the abyss of war,
carried it across mountains of madness.
They were unable to wrest it from you,
resurrection-woman

Share with me, your daughter,
you who know,
unbowed
against the atheism
of the weapons' forests
and shameless golden calves
your deep knowledge:
how to resist
God-lessness.

9. God is just
— and no opium

The cross,
says our brother bishop
with his golden cross
on his purple front,
is at the centre
of our life.

The cross,
I say,
is more likely
to mark the end
of our life.

On Calvary,
in Flossenbürg,
El Salvador.

Risk
of God's love of people
or people's love of God
in which I believe
more strongly
than in anything else.

Alternative exposition of
Philippians 2:5-8

Misuse of the Christian religion

How is it that words like justice and justification are so
central in the Bible, and yet churches and Christians have on the
whole bothered so little about justice in the world?

I must admit that during my theological training I spent
hours, days, weeks, months and years trying to understand the
meaning of justification and God's justice without ever linking
them with the injustice I participated in, or committed, or was
subjected to. Maybe it was my historical heritage which had
made me accustomed to read the Bible through Romans 3-8
spectacles, and to judge all other texts in the light of that: do
they have anything to say about the justification of sinners
through faith? At the time, the Christian faith always seemed to
me to be more a matter of a spiritual attitude than of a way of
life.

I was once very disturbed about something a woman from El
Salvador said to me, almost crying: "I so long to speak as a

churchwoman, but the only thing I can voice is the cry: we want justice!" Another example of this contrast between church and justice!

Reactionary political forces all over the world these days are making use of Christian groups and revival movements and even of influential church leaders in order to defame those who are devoting their life to greater social justice, by branding them as communists and Marxists. And many Christians are just standing by as if they were merely spectators. Is it possible to have a spectator's attitude towards those who with theological arguments are trying to persuade the people that the Bible has nothing to do with justice, that one cannot change the world anyway, and thus defame all those who are struggling for social justice as non-Christian? That ought to please the oppressors!

There is a comment by Napoleon Bonaparte which makes this state of affairs unmistakably clear:

> As far as I am concerned, what I see in religion is not the mystery of the Incarnation but a mystery of the social order: it prevents the rich from being massacred by the poor by relating the idea of equality to heaven...
>
> Priests are worth more than Kant and all the German dreamers put together. Without religion, how could we have order in the state? Society cannot continue to exist without inequalities of personal fortunes; for inequalities to continue we must have religion. When someone is dying of hunger and someone else nearby has everything, it would be impossible for the starving man to acquiesce to disparity if there were no authority to tell him: God wills it so; in this world there must be rich and poor but in the hereafter for all eternity, fortunes will be reversed. [51]

What are we to make of all this? A great deal of our spiritual heritage is characterized by the division between soul and world. We find this also deeply ingrained in our liturgical language.

There is the attitude of "individualistic salvation" (*Heilsegoismus*). There is a dualistic world-view by which the present world is discredited as provisional over against the real world which is yet to come. There is the discouragement of and diversion away from an active Christian life-style by a speculative theology which is being "cooked up" in sound-proof ivory towers.

It was at the Fourth Assembly of the World Council of Churches in Uppsala in 1968 that the biblical texts about justice were for me for the first time ever brought into relationship with reality. The theological laboratory called "oikoumene" had gritted the normally so slippery discussions about justice with the sand of earthiness. Here was a church organization expressing itself about proper, earthy, concrete justice. True, it was not the first time for it to do so, but I did not know that at the time. For me it was a genuine conversion experience; I could hardly "believe" it!

In these latter stages of the twentieth century the World Council of Churches will more than ever need to fulfill that role of being such a laboratory. Reactionary politics are becoming stronger everywhere, church conservatism is spreading, the world economy is in a state of extreme imbalance, dangerous technological manipulation is being applied all the time, and in addition to it all there is the constant threat of a nuclear holocaust. What we need more than anything is the clear unequivocal affirmation that the Bible is not silent in the face of the world's injustice. Injustice is a denial of the covenant between God and human beings.

There are already enough drug addicts. Religion should not ever again be the opium that transports us into a spiritual cloud-cuckoo land while we are all the time wandering around the world in a pious trance. In fact, what we need today is a kind of Programme to Combat the Misuse of the Christian Religion. The covenant between God and human beings of which the Bible speaks is being contradicted by the way Christians obscure reality and abdicate from the world.

The vision of the kingdom of God, in which justice will dwell, still weighs more heavily with me than star wars and the catastrophe of starvation on earth. What else do we have left to believe in, and to cause us to hope, except that our strength under God's hands becomes so large and strong and convincing, that the world will *not* slide into the abyss? What else do we have left except to work, pray and think accordingly?

Or should we meanwhile have become exponents of the dinosaur theory according to which everyone, man/woman included, will ultimately have to become extinct?

Justice, peace and the integrity of creation, as we said at the Sixth Assembly of the World Council of Churches, are the preferred solutions, because they are biblical. What is the meaning of the individual salvation of the soul, unless it is embedded in that larger vision of the wellbeing and the redemption of all people, of the whole of creation, in God's great shalom?

Each day we can make a new start, so the Old and New Testaments teach us. We do, in fact, have the choice to return to the covenant, to re-erect the fallen signposts. It is never too late, and every grain of sand thrown into the works of the machine of death may be able to bring it to a halt.

God's justice at the heart of the Bible

Justice — the Bible refers to it everywhere. People throughout the centuries have been bringing their vision, their variations on this main theme, as prayed and echoed in their life, and have contributed all this to one great symphony.

God's justice was talked about by that wandering shepherd Abraham and his rejected, pregnant slave girl Hagar — she was the first woman who had something to say about this. Pitiful shepherd tribes in Israel spoke about it, as did the cunning midwives in Egypt, who by their lies saved the lives of children. It was of justice that those slave people spoke as they found their way towards freedom — judges, kings and prophets. An apprehensive virgin called Mary asked after justice, and so did Galilean shepherds and fishermen, Jews and gentiles, and Paul, the tent-maker.

The vision of God's justice has shaped the face of the earth throughout the ages, and came to life in the history of humankind, as varied as life itself; it was heard from the mouth of children, women, rabbis, labourers, philosophers, lawyers, musicians, theologians. At the same time this vision was watered down, diluted, distorted, but also, it was newly discovered, cleansed, spelled out afresh, lived out and passed on from one generation to the next. Also to us. We are part of a human chain of tenacious and hopeful people, a chain that makes us strong and shows us where we are going.

Somewhere, on a side road of our Jewish-Christian tradition, I came across a little story, from that great eighteenth-century renewal movement among the East European Jews, the Chassidim. "After Yom Kippur the Rabbi of Berdichev sent for a tailor and asked him to report on how his disputes with God had gone the previous day. The tailor said: 'I told God: You want me to repent of my sins, but I have only committed slight transgressions. Maybe I have stolen a little left-over cloth, or eaten in a non-Jewish home without washing my hands after working there. But you, Lord, have committed great sins: you have taken away little children from their mothers, and mothers from their little children. Let us call it quits: you forgive me and I will forgive you.'"[52]

Is there really such a thing as God's balancing justice? Say something terrible happens: cancer, the death of a loved one, unemployment, the break-up of a love, a tragic accident, a child who becomes a drug addict, poverty, defamation or the hatred someone heaps up against you. Then that question springs up: "Why? Why me? Why so hard? Have I then done such a wicked thing in my life?" That is what Job, too, asked in the Bible.

Such people, who after all are so much like ourselves, are sitting with God at the negotiating table, asking for justice and fairness. But was there ever any such deal with God guaranteeing us an undisturbed life and happiness? Is there a court of justice one could appeal to? And anyway: is God a kind of computer specialist who sits at some keyboard and arbitrarily presses the keys of our destiny? Is God in the Bible really such an infinitely omnipotent superman, about whom in the Middle Ages Thomas Aquinas pondered so deeply, and whom the philosopher Ockham gave the final philosophical legitimation?

If the tailor in the story is just a clever book-keeper, good at figures, who stakes his rightful claim with a potentate on the other side, who exercises an arbitrary rule, then this is a very straightforward story. It follows the rules of the capitalist game: you give me so much — I will give you so much in return. It has absolutely nothing to do with God's justice. But the story points in another direction. When we follow it closely, we get right back to the beginning, to the moment of birth of God's justice.

Between the tailor and God in this story there is a deep mutual trust; they are like neighbours who are also good friends. God is not a far-away God, but has a human face; you can talk with God without fear. The tailor knows God's friendship. Both make mistakes and suffer bad luck. The tailor does not address his complaints to some distant all-powerful ruler, but here are two closely related partners, talking with each other and forgiving one another. The tailor takes the liberty of reminding God of their common history. This kind of open, frank conversational interplay between a human being and God is hardly known in our Protestant theology. Such a close relationship can only exist where the people and God have something in common, namely a mutual commitment. This comes out even more clearly in the latter part of the story where the Rabbi of Berdichev says to the tailor: "Why did you let God get away with it so lightly?" Only people who really trust the commitment God has given them are able to talk like that.

And so this story takes us back to the cradle of all our knowledge about justice, to that overwhelming promise, to that great covenant between God and the people on Mount Sinai (Ex. 19:1-25). It was in a desert, in which many more covenants were going to be solemnized, that an escaped bunch of runaway slaves under a determined leader, plagued by hunger and thirst, but at least free — free! — put their trust in this Yahweh, a God of liberation.

To these half-hearted, freed people in their vulnerability, Yahweh made a promise to journey with them, to be totally committed to them, to their rescue, their salvation. This is God's first declaration of love for humanity: God wants to be a protector of those who are the most helpless of all, the orphans, widows, those who mourn, the have-nots.

In the sheer joy of their new-found freedom, the people commit themselves totally to this God, who appears in burning bushes, who divides the waters, and who has introduced them to a new life — away from slavery in Egypt.

Those who have thus been liberated promise to protect each other, as Yahweh had done, not to steal from each other or kill one another, not to spread lies, not to rob others of their property. Ten basic rules for life — that is all we need. Moses inscribes them on the tablets of stone (Ex. 20:1-17).

But first and foremost, people simply committed themselves to this Yahweh, covenanting with this One who had saved their life, and who had shown them how to live. And God pleads with them, as do all the prophets: Choose life! (Deut. 30:15-20). It is not true that everything is already predetermined; we are not doomed to destruction. God gives us a free choice — people can decide which way to go, any time. Israel had a name for it: God is just. It is not a matter of quality, but rather one of how God acts. It is not a matter of characteristics but a promise — not to the individual soul, but to a whole community, to all people together.

That is not only how it will be between God and human beings, but also among human beings themselves. The way they live reflects, communicates who their God is. Justice and existing for each other confirm this. "I shall be there as the one who will be there." God is there for the people and they in turn are there for God and for each other.

The ten words of life were the signposts, planted generously in the landscape of life to protect people's togetherness. These commandments were reasonable, understandable, realistic. That is how Yahweh's covenant people should live. Nevertheless, these rules are not placed in history like irksome obstacles; they were only signposts. As the desert nomads entered into new realms of living, they expressed God's will in new formulations adapted to their new circumstances, but never without relating them to the earlier signposts of the desert.

In their hymns, the psalms, the Jewish people sing of the manifold character of God's justice. Over and over again, they sing about the covenant, and the memory of how it all started is rekindled. God's justice and the wellbeing of the people are inextricably linked together; heaven and earth combine to raise the fruit, a child born of peace and justice:

> Deliverance is near to those who worship him, so that glory may dwell in our land. Love and fidelity have come together; justice and peace join hands. Fidelity springs up from the earth and justice looks down from heaven. The Lord will add prosperity, and our land shall yield its harvest. Justice shall go in front of him and the path before him shall be peace (Ps. 85:10-14).

Keeping the covenant means ensuring right relationships among the people. Only then will shalom, peace, salvation, liberation, faithfulness, truth, trust, confidence in each other come together — all this marks God's justice and the relationship with the people. [53]

The tailor in the story reminds God of their mutual agreement. Such extraordinary familiarity and mutuality grow and come together out of this long history of the covenant.

However, time and time again, after being freed, after the allegiance sworn in the desert, there are moments of betrayal and persistent rebelliousness, and of people's inability to keep their promises.

It results in the break-up of the community. The poor, widows, orphans are neglected, foreigners are maltreated, property is stolen and accumulated while others are starving. Foreign powers attack Israel and destroy its heritage. The prophets issue warnings and call people to repentance, but in vain. God's word, the life-giving Torah, is manipulated and twisted until in the end it is narrowed down to a set of pedantic interpretations and religious rites, missing the true meaning of the covenant, and just leaving empty phrases behind.

God is left behind as a betrayed lover, whose beloved chose to go after someone else, after other interests, golden calves, mammon and power, rituals, splendour and pious busy-ness. With a human heart, God is angry and sad. The great promise — turned down; justice — betrayed and despised; loyalty, truth and trust — suppressed. God watches the people as they rush into disaster, as wars are started, with their resulting atrocities. "For sin pays a wage, and the wage is death", says Paul (Rom. 6:23). And God weeps, weeps over Jerusalem and over all of us (Luke 19:41).

If things had gone on as they generally do when agreements and promises are broken — between two people, between business partners, between peoples and nations — they would have become really tough. Arguments, swords would have been sharpened, court proceedings instituted and missiles stationed. But, as the Bible says, God remains faithful to those who betray the covenant. God does not stop carrying out his/her share in the commitment; going as far as it is possible to go. God puts on human clothing, surrounded with a human smell, is born as a human baby in a manger, and comes to those who have lost a sense of the divine presence, living as they do, in conditions of extreme poverty. God takes this action to prove that justice in people's lives *is* possible, that forgiveness and love *can* be lived out and practised in the world as it is.

The broken covenant, the break-down in relationships will be restored through God taking one-sided initiatives towards God's people, as well as through people taking first steps towards each other.

This is God's second great declaration of love to humanity: in the person of Jesus God enters into all the dirt of our human-ness, but this time it is not just a case of the one suffering for his own people. He suffers also for foreigners, for Canaanites, Samaritans and all gentiles, yes, for the whole inhabited world, the oikoumene. And it is precisely in the dirt of human history that it becomes clear what God's justice is all about: going out to find unfaithful covenant partners, not giving up the search for the lost coin. God is just, in that he/she turns his/her face towards the weak, towards the poor in spirit, those who hunger and thirst for righteousness/justice, the peace-makers. God's justice is so great that it seeks to abolish enmity, and proves it by turning the other cheek — and not only the other cheek but all of life itself. That is how we know that God's justice bears the name of grace and mercy (Matt. 5-7: the Sermon on the Mount).

Jesus spoke about this justice by using a new language. He called it the kingdom of God which he wanted to bring about. Thus the two became synonymous: justice is the hallmark of God's kingdom. And what Jesus did confirmed what he said. And so he became the basic model of a life dedicated to this kingdom of God and its righteousness. He opened the door through which many in the course of the centuries were to follow him. People of all times have drawn their faith and strength for living from it and modelled their lives on it. By human standards, his life was a disaster. It ended in the utter terror of the gallows. "Serves him right," thinks the realist, sitting back. Standing up for God's justice had for Jesus the brutal consequence of being killed. His death sentence was carried out through hate, fear, political cowardice and religious fanaticism.

The far-reaching misunderstanding of the empty cross

The early church was quick to interpret the death of Jesus by using the symbolism of the Jewish Passover (Heb. 9:11-10:18: the once-and-for-all sacrifice of Christ). Here, someone was sacrificed for the whole people, but it had to be seen as the final and complete sacrifice, made once and for all. An end to cutting hearts out of human bodies, as the Aztecs used to do on their altars. No more killing of people because some are screaming: String him/her up! No more lynchings, scapegoats, arch-enemies. The last sacrifice has been made, once and for all.

But at the same time a terribly far-reaching misunderstanding crept into the church's thinking. Alongside the bold and world-shaking message of the Easter morning: "Life triumphs over death, the God of the Bible no longer needs death-rites; no more human sacrifices", a convenient thought was slipped in. On the one hand, the conclusion was drawn that one should believe this and commit oneself to ensure that no one should ever again be sacrificed to pacify whatever God or human being. On the other hand, there had to be the readiness to sacrifice oneself, and be crucified to defend this truth. And these are two very different things. The first concerns others being sacrificed, the second affects my own life. The sacrifice of Jesus, "once and for all", could so easily become an excuse for trying to avoid the consequences for oneself. "Christ loves in our stead... the estranged 'faith' in Christ is a substitute for the 'Imitatio Christi'". [54] It was a great temptation for the church to preach empty crosses on which it was no longer prepared to put its own life. The cross of Jesus could be lifted up as a religious symbol without facing the dangerous challenge, that the implementation of "Never again human sacrifices; God has been reconciled" might well call for one's own crucifixion.

And where people are so slow to recognize the need for this willingness, the symbol becomes dead and empty, and it is then no longer possible to see any reality that is meant to coincide with the sign. (Symbol, from the Greek verb "symballein", literally means to fall or be thrown together, to be in communication with each other.) We have turned the "folly of the cross" (1 Cor. 1:18) into something empty, something trivial: ornaments on purple cassocks, religious arts and crafts exuding religious sentiment. What in the world does this have to do with what Jesus said: "If anyone wishes to be a follower of mine, he/she must leave self behind; he/she must take up his/her cross and come with me" (Matt. 16:24)? Such a saying has nothing whatsoever in common with a pious veneration of the cross, nor is it a challenge to throw oneself heroically into suffering, nor a call to bear whatever suffering may come like a little lamb. On the contrary — what Jesus says is a call deliberately and with one's eyes wide open to accept a risk.

Nowadays we are learning afresh that in every human being who is innocently sacrificed God is insulted and crucified, and that every human being who gives up his/her life for others participates in this mystery of the life and death of Jesus. The grain of wheat that falls to the ground gives rise to new life through death. Ita Ford, a Catholic nun, was murdered in El Salvador as a direct result of the sin of genocide committed against the indigenous people. Elisabeth Käsemann, that very committed young German woman, was murdered in Argentina as a direct result of the sin of militarism. These women risked and gave up their lives for the poor. Dietrich Bonhoeffer died for others as a direct result of the sin of our fathers' and mothers' fascism. The way they gave their life can only be seen as "Imitatio Christi". In sacrifices like these, God's justice breaks through, and puts many people on the same track again. "There is no greater love than this, that a man/woman should lay down his/her life for his/her friends," says Jesus. In the light of this, the cross can hardly remain an empty symbol!

It is at this very point that God's holiness enters into our contemporary reality. In the ecumenical movement we keep experiencing that people live out their own life and their struggle for the poor in the light of this symbol.

Many artistic expressions have grown out of this. The crucified Christ has a black skin, he wears the overalls of a Korean labourer, he wears the poncho and has the facial features of a Central American Indian, he screams with the screams of those tortured in Argentina. Such interpretations of the cross in the idioms of today can be seen on the walls of many a church office. They are proclaiming that God is still being crucified.

But what an uproar there was when some time ago there was a woman among those who were being crucified today! An

American sculptress in a modern crucifixion scene once portrayed a crucified woman.[55] For many, that was too much of a
theological challenge. Is it more difficult to cope with than
when Jesus is black? Have not women throughout the ages been
crucified, tortured, killed because of their faith? Are they not at
the present time being battered, raped, sold, humiliated? Is the
suffering they endure not worth being related to the suffering of
Jesus? Do they not also give their life for others? Or does the
refusal to make this connection signify that women's lives are
after all of no value, that their self-sacrifice does not reflect
Jesus' sacrifice, and that they do not bear God's likeness? One
has to think long and hard about this kind of provocation. For
when women today do reject the cross as a symbol, it is partly
due to the fact that the church has so consistently ignored their
crucifixions. It would be more appropriate for the church to
adopt an attitude of penitence than one of being judgmental.
Thoughts like these can only serve to bring us to a more
profound examination of religious symbolism and its rootedness
in history. Symbol and reality belong inextricably together. It
seems to me, though, that in the area of God's justice there is an
enormous gap between a pious veneration of the cross and the
willingness to take up the cross as a consequence of our struggle
for God's kingdom in a world that knows no mercy. We know
ourselves only too well, including our countless cowardices of
which we are guilty every day.

When people are no longer reminded of the historical meaning of the cross, where empty crosses are being proclaimed,
where our thoughtlessness lays crosses on others, where we are
no longer able to identify the most violent crucifixions of people
today in our own familiar context, we are surrendering the cross
to be masochistically abused by all those misguided people who
see suffering in everything. Or they cause suffering to others,
and then pretend that this is what Christianity is all about.
Throughout the ages, the church has far too often allowed the
meaning of the cross to degenerate in this way.

In El Salvador, there is a church cooperative, where they
carve and paint crosses. They are happy crosses.[56] At the top
you can see the sun, on the cross-beam a flower, a house, a bird.
On the upright beam a dove, a small dwelling. All of it is
painted in cheerful colours and radiates a happy, peasant sim-

plicity: a cross of life, a tree of life revealing what is to come despite the agony, where we are going — into a new life, into creation itself, into fellowship. Those are the gifts of the Spirit. I am deeply grateful to the Christians in El Salvador, where today — God knows — enough people are being crucified, that they are liberating me from my theological imprisonment, for there is also about my understanding of the cross not much that is green and holding life's promise. Their happy cross stands in front of me as a challenge in future to think more deeply about its meaning.

The "folly of the cross" is part and parcel of that divine attempt to restore justice between God and humanity, and also within the human community. It is as if we are touched, and "infected" with justice. God passes on to us his/her passion for people. Paul, in his complex way of speaking, calls that "justification of sinners by faith". Yes, I have already spoken much about sins: there are so many of them — personal sins, corporate and structural sins. All of them are in need of purification and cleansing.

All those who separate the sinner's justification by faith as a legalistic personal process from the content and compassion of God's justice, have introduced "a tragic misunderstanding of righteousness — justice, (as having been) the ideological instrument for divorcing faith from love, dogmatics and ethics, God's grace and man's responsibility", as Miguez-Bonino of Argentina puts it. [57]

Only a badly misunderstood Luther can be appealed to as justifying such a divorce. After all, is not this what it says in the letter to the Romans: "It is not by hearing the law, but by doing it that men/women will be justified before God... Does this mean that we are using faith to undermine law? By no means: we are placing law itself on a firmer footing" (Rom. 2:13 and 3:31).

If it is true that Jesus is the true unambiguous image of God, and if the thirty years of his life are not an exceptional temporary assignment of being God-on-earth, then we are seeing God completely differently from an infinite, all-mighty ruler — who to me seems to be rather the projection of male power fantasies anyway. Holding power over life and death must almost be a fascinating kind of intoxication, much in the same way as we see the super-powers of today enacting it in a terrifying real drama. But that does not mean that God is therefore powerless; God's power is simply of a different order. It is, as I have mentioned before, that irresistible power of unarmed truth, of wholly devoted love, and of a clearly focused justice. These are the ingredients of a totally different type of omnipotence. The sharp and prophetic critique which Jesus exercised arose out of a compassionate heart and a clearly focused love. This is the only thing Jesus possesses by way of power — it is the only power we, too, will have, if we follow him.

What will you do? — "I'm gon' stand!"

Where do we find the strength to be as bold as this? Where in the world? It is vital to draw upon all possible reserves in soul, brain and body, both individually, and also — preferably — corporately, within our churches. To do this we need to mobilize the deepest spiritual forces that sustain, strengthen and motivate us. We receive strength from outside sources too, from others, from God. Bonhoeffer, my never-tiring, faithful witness, was one of those who was able to draw on all his inner resources in order to become a man of resistance. For as is the case with theology, so in the area of spirituality we are running the danger of losing the dialectical tension between "resistance and submission". Bonhoeffer was an exponent of the fact that resistance is born out of spirituality and community life. His resistance arose from the very depth of his spiritual roots. It was he who as early as 1935 identified as the church's principal task the struggle against racism, social injustice and war (and I would add sexism), as a sign of obedience to God, rather than as a self-selected priority.[58] He was also the one who, as a result of spiritual and intellectual experience of resistance, was capable of surrendering his life into the hands of God. The doctor who witnessed his death said afterwards that he had never seen anyone die in such surrender to God. Among the workers for justice there is a great deal of true piety. I have met many of them who have stepped out of spirituality into resistance. Otherwise they would not have been able to withstand.

I must admit that often the words of our traditional hymns and prayers stick in my throat, for they have lost that tension between resistance and submission.

Our spiritual language tends to train us more for submission than for resistance. But the spiritual sources for a life of courageous confrontation need to flow richly if we are not to get lost in bitterness and resignation.

In dealing with the issue of God's justice I have learned a lot from the "brethren". But spiritually, I have been, and continue to be, sustained by the songs of the black sisters "Sweet Honey in the Rock". Maybe the spiritual force of what they have to say does not come across as powerfully in the printed word as it does in the sound of their voices and their lively appearance. They who are singing "Oh Lord, hold my hand while I run this race, I'm your child while I run this race", are singing for me and for all, the enduring litany of practising God's justice for his/her world:

> We will not bow down to racism!
> We will not bow down to injustice!
> We will not bow down to exploitation!
>
> I'm gon' stand! I'm gon' stand!
>
> We just can't tolerate racism!
> We just can't tolerate injustice!
> We just can't tolerate exploitation!
>
> I'm gon' stand! I'm gon' stand!
>
> We will not obey racism!
> We will not obey injustice!
> We will not obey exploitation!
>
> I'm gon' stand! I'm gon' stand!

Notes

1. *Child of the Dark: The Diary of Carolina Maria de Jesus,* New York: New American Library, 1964.

2. Position paper on "Feminist Theology," by the bishops of the North Elbe Province, 1 July 1985.

3. Text of the record: Eva Maria Hagen/Wolf Biermann, "Nicht Liebe ohne Liebe" (Not Love without Love), 1979.

4. This phrase comes from the Russian philosopher Nikolai Berdyaev.

5. Quoted by Erich Fromm, cf. *You Shall Be as Gods: A Radical Interpretation of the Old Testament and Its Tradition,* New York: Holt, Rinehart and Winston, 1966, pp. 54–55.

6. Poster of the Rogation Action by the Evangelisches Missionswerk, Hamburg.

7. This is how I understand that often wrongly used passage in Hebrews 12:4–11: "For the Lord disciplines whom he loves. At the moment when any discipline is applied it appears not so much to lead to joy as to sadness; it is not until later that it gives to those who have been trained by it a peaceful harvest of justice."

8. Leonardo Boff, *Way of the Cross — Way of Justice,* Maryknoll, N.Y.: Orbis Books, 1980.

9. Wolf Biermann, *Verdrehte Welt — das seh'ich gerne,* Cologne, 1982, p. 21.

10. This phrase by Suzanne de Dietrich was passed on to me only verbally.

11. From Kurt Marti, *Geduld und Revolte, die Gedichte am Rande,* Stuttgart: Radius, 1984.

12. Christa Reinig, as quoted by Karl-Josef Kuschel, in his *Gottesbilder-Menschenbilder,* Zürich, 1985, p. 70.

13. Friedrich Hölderlin, *Collected Works,* ed. Friedrich Beissner, Frankfurt, 1965, p. 239.

14. Christoph Blumhardt, in *Ansprachen, Predigten, Reden, Briefe, 1865–1917,* vol. 3, Neukirchen-Vluyn, 1978, p. 1.

15. The confessional documents of the Evangelical Lutheran Church, Göttingen, 1963, CA VII, p. 61.

16. I have taken this thought from Boris Pasternak's book, *Doctor Zhivago,* where it appears thus: "The irresistible power of unarmed truth, the attraction of its example" (London: Fontana Monarchs, 1958, p. 49).

17. This and following quotes are taken from the record: "We All, Everyone of Us."

18. Dietrich Bonhoeffer, *Letters and Papers from Prison,* London: SCM Press, 1967, p. 346.

19. Ibid., p. 15.

20. EPD (Evangelischer Pressedienst), 20 September 1982. Statement by the Council of the EKD (Evangelische Kirche in Deutschland).

21. IDEA (Informationsdienst der Evangelischen Allianz), 12 September 1983. Statement by Gerhard Mayer, rector of the Albrecht Bengel House.

22. Bonhoeffer, *Letters and Papers from Prison,* p. 6.

23. After an Erich Fried saying.

24. Allan Boesak at the Sixth Assembly of the World Council of Churches, Vancouver, 1983.

25. Jacques Lusseyran, *Das wiedergefundene Licht,* Hamburg, 1963, pp. 7f. Eng. trans.: *And There Was Light,* Boston, Little, Brown, 1963.

26. Bonhoeffer, *Letters and Papers from Prison,* p. 300.

27. Eberhard Bethge, *Am gegebenen Ort: Aufsätze u. Reden 1970–1979,* Munich, 1979, p. 47.

28. *Wir sind keine Fremdlinge mehr* (No Longer Strangers), women engage in worship, Hamburg, 1984, p. 51.

29. Position paper on feminist theology (see note 2).

30. Rosemary Radford Ruether, "Of One Humanity," in *Sojourners,* January 1984, p. 17. The following passage also contains thoughts from the anthology *Feminist Interpretation of the Bible,* ed. Letty Russell, Philadelphia: Westminster Press, 1985, especially from Rosemary Radford Ruether's "Feminist Interpretation: A Method of Correlation," pp. 111–124.

31. Position paper (see note 2).

32. Augustine, *City of God,* ed. David Knowles, Penguin Books, 1972, XIX, from chaps. 16–24, pp. 577–598. "In fact, to put it briefly, in the punishment of that sin the retribution for disobedience is simply disobedience itself. For man's wretchedness is nothing but his own disobedience to himself, so that because he would not do what he could, he now wills what he cannot.... It may be objected that the flesh is in such a state that it cannot serve our will ... our flesh, which had been subject to us, now gives us trouble through its non-compliance, whereas we by our defiance of God only succeeded in becoming a nuisance to ourselves.... This (sexual) lust assumes power not only over the whole body ... it disturbs the whole man, when the mental emotion combines and mingles with the physical craving, resulting in a pleasure surpassing all physical delight.... Sometimes the (sexual) impulse is an unwanted intruder, sometimes it abandons the eager lover, and desire cools off in the body while it

is at boiling heat in the mind. Thus strangely does lust refuse to be a servant not only to the will to beget but even to the lust for lascivious indulgence; and although on the whole it is totally opposed to the mind's control, it is quite often divided against itself.... Then (had there been no sin) the man would have sowed the seed and the women would have conceived the child when their sexual organs had been aroused by the will, at the appropriate time and in the necessary degree, and had not been excited by lust.... If this is so, is there any reason why we should not believe that before the sin of disobedience and its punishment of corruptibility, the members of a man's body could have been servants of man's will without any lust, for the procreation of children?... Hence came the more obvious misery when man does not live as he wishes to live. If he lived as he wished, he would consider himself happy...."

33. Domitila B. de Chungara, *Let Me Speak! Testimony of Domitila, a Woman of the Bolivian Tin Mines,* New York: Monthly Review Press, 1979.

34. Rigoberta Menchu, *I, Rigoberta Menchu,* London, Verso, 1984.

35. Bonhoeffer, *Letters and Papers from Prison,* pp. 381f.

36. Roger Garaudy, *Der letzte Ausweg, Feminisierung der Gesellschaft* (Feminization of society), Olten, 1982, p. 37.

37. Wolfgang Roth and Rosemary Radford Ruether, *The Liberating Bond: Covenants Biblical and Contemporary,* New York: Friendship Press, 1978, pp. 68f.

38. Irmtraud Morgner, *Die Hexe im Landhaus, Gespräch in Solothurn,* Zürich, 1984, pp. 54ff.

39. In 1911, the Massachusetts legislature passed a law limiting the working hours of women and children to 54 hours per week. The textile corporation, in retaliation for this workers' victory, then cut *all* employees' hours to 54 per week, with a corresponding reduction in wages. The workers in the textile mills began a nine-week strike on 1 January 1912. Some 20,000 people took part in a protest march in which women workers carried banners: "Bread and Roses"; they fought not only for workers' rights, but for the quality of life. James Oppenheim subsequently wrote the text of this song which has become a leitmotif for the struggle by women, students and workers for greater justice.

40. Martin Buber, *Eclipse of God,* London: Victor Gollancz, 1953, pp. 16, 17, 18.

41. Hölderlin, *Collected Works,* p. 239.

42. Bonhoeffer, *Letters and Papers from Prison,* p. 360.

43. Suzanne de Dietrich, *Was Gott mit uns vorhat,* Basel, 1967, p. 81, where she summarizes the exegetical discussion of this passage along Gerhard von Rad's line, as taken in his *Old Testament Theology.*

44. Declaration by the Kirchliche Sammlung um Bibel und Bekenntnis, *Welt am Sonntag,* 6 September 1981.

45. Rainer Maria Rilke, *Duino Elegies,* Hogarth Press, 1948, p. 91.

46. Philippians 2:6, "... he did not think to snatch at equality with God, but made himself nothing, assuming the nature of a slave. Bearing the human likeness, revealed in human shape, he humbled himself...."

47. Schalom Ben Chorin, *Jüdischer Glaube,* Tübingen, 1979, pp. 88ff.

48. 1 Corinthians 3:16,17: "Surely, you know that you are God's temple, where the spirit of God dwells. Anyone who destroys God's temple will himself be destroyed by God, because the temple of God is holy and that temple you are."

49. Gioconda Belli, *Feuerlinie,* poems, Wuppertal, 1981, p. 20.

50. Matthew 25:31–46: The final judgment. In this passage Jesus speaks of those who do his will without being conscious of it: "Lord, when was it that we saw you hungry and fed you, or thirsty and gave you drink?... I tell you this; anything you did for one of my brothers (or sisters) here, however humble, you did for me."

51. Quoted from Georges Casalis in Virginia Fabella and Sergio Torres, eds., *Doing Theology in a Divided World,* Maryknoll, N.Y.: Orbis Books, 1985, p. 111.

52. Quoted by Erich Fromm, cf. *You Shall Be as Gods,* p. 152.

53. Philip Potter: "Blessed are those who hunger and thirst for righteousness," in *And Yet Happy: The Beatitudes Revisited,* Geneva: WSCF Books, 1981.

54. Erich Fromm, *Gesamtwerk,* vol. 2, Stuttgart, 1980. p. 371.

55. *New York,* 30 April 1984, p. 13, "Female Christ on display."

56. *Jesus Christ, the Life of the World,* worship book for the Sixth Assembly of the World Council of Churches, 1983, p. 42.

57. José Míguez-Bonino, *Towards a Christian Political Ethics,* Philadelphia: Fortress, 1983, p. 124.

58. Bonhoeffer, *Gesammelte Schriften,* ed. E. Bethge, vol. 1, Munich, 1958, p. 261.

Also from Meyer • Stone Books...

AGAINST MACHISMO
**Rubem Alves, Leonardo Boff, Gustavo Gutiérrez,
José Míguez Bonino, Juan Luis Segundo...
and Others
Talk About the Struggle of Women**

Interviews by Elsa Tamez

The seeds of liberation theology grew out of the oppression of the poor. Now, leading liberation theologians, some for the first time, speak out on the oppression of women.

With unusual vision, Elsa Tamez poses prodding questions that evoke both the issues and the experience of these individuals. Her exploration of the reality of women's struggle, the relationship between women and the church, the contribution of women to theology, and the dramatic influence of feminist hermeneutics results in diverse and searching conversation that breaks new ground.

There is a richness to these interviews that stems from the interview genre itself. These are not formal statements buttressed by footnotes, but rather the personal, spontaneous, insightful, wrestled reflections, feelings, and experiences of Latin America's leading liberation theologians.

Elsa Tamez is Professor of Biblical Studies at the Seminario Bíblico Latinoamericano in Costa Rica.

Theology/Feminist Studies   160 pp.

Hardcover: $24.95 (ISBN 0-940989-13-1)
Paperback: $9.95 (ISBN 0-940989-12-3)

WOMANPRAYER, WOMANSONG
Resources for Ritual

Miriam Therese Winter

Illustrated by Meinrad Craighead

" . . . a groundbreaking contribution. This exciting book addresses the urgent need for ritual which incorporates women's experience. Feminine biblical images of God are recovered; feminine pronouns for God are supplied; valiant women are remembered; the church year is reinterpreted to highlight women's experience; and oppression and violence against women in scripture and society are exposed. I have found a rich resource here!"
— Ruth Duck, Editor, *Everflowing Streams*

"For the first time the church prays and sings the ancient story of creation and redemption through women's creative imagination."   — Rosemary Ruether

Miriam Therese Winter is Professor of Liturgy, Worship, and Spirituality at Hartford Seminary, Hartford, Connecticut. She is the author of *Why Sing? Toward a Theology of Catholic Church Music.*

Feminist Studies/Liturgy   264 pp.

Paperback: $14.95 (ISBN 0-940989-00-X)

LIBERATION THEOLOGY
Essential Facts about the Revolutionary Religious Movement in Latin America and Beyond

Phillip Berryman

"Phillip Berryman writes clearly and convincingly about what may turn out to be the most important religious movement since the Protestant Reformation. Persuasive and provocative, *Liberation Theology* should be read by everyone who wants to understand the preferential option for the poor and the spiritual revolutions going on in Latin America."
— Robert F. Drinan

"...just the book I've been searching for. As the basic text for my course on liberation theology, it is everything I need: concise, well written, balanced. It gives some real attention to the critics of liberation theology, which any fair text must do."
— Harvey Cox

Phillip Berryman is the author of *The Religious Roots of Rebellion* and *Inside Central America*.

Theology 240 pp.

Paperback: ISBN 0-940989-03-4, $6.95

*Order from your bookstore
or from
Meyer • Stone Books
1821 West Third Street, Bloomington, IN 47401
Tel.: 812-333-0313*